The Supporters' Guide

to

Premier &
Football League
Clubs
2008

EDITOR
John Robinson

Twenty-fourth Edition

CONTENTS

British Library Cataloguing in Publication Data
A catalogue record for this book is available from the British Library

ISBN: 978-1-86223-158-0

Copyright © 2007, SOCCER BOOKS LIMITED (01472 696226)
72 St. Peter's Avenue, Cleethorpes, N.E. Lincolnshire, DN35 8HU, England
Web site   http://www.soccer-books.co.uk
e-mail   info@soccer-books.co.uk

The Publishers, and the Football Clubs itemised are unable to accept liability for any loss, damage or injury caused by error or inaccuracy in the information published in this guide.

Manufactured in the UK by LPPS Ltd, Wellingborough, NN8 3PJ

FOREWORD

We are indebted to the staffs of the clubs featured in this guide for their cooperation and also to Michael Robinson (page layouts), Bob Budd (cover artwork) and Tony Brown (Cup Statistics – www.soccerdata.com).

When using this guide, please note that 'child' concessions also include senior citizens unless stated otherwise. Some clubs had not fixed their matchday admission prices at the time of going to press and in these cases we have had to use the 2006/2007 prices in the absence of new information. It should be noted that although actual matchday admission prices are shown in this guide, many clubs offer discounts for tickets purchased before the day of the game.

Disabled Supporters' information is once again included in the guide and, to ensure that facilities are not overstretched, we recommend that disabled fans pre-book wherever possible.

Regular purchasers of the guide will notice that we have included a number of new ground photographs in this edition. Ground moves and redevelopment are continuing apace and travelling fans may find that away sections and prices change during the course of the 2007/2008 season. If any readers have alternative ground photos which they would like us to consider for insertion in future issues, they should write to me care of the address opposite.

Finally, we would like to wish our readers a happy and safe spectating season.

John Robinson
EDITOR

WEMBLEY STADIUM

First Opened: 1923 (Re-opened in 2007 after rebuild)
Address: Wembley National Stadium, Wembley,
London   HA9 0WS
Correspondence: P.O.Box 1966, London, SW1P 3EQ
Telephone Nº: 0844 980-8001
Fax Number: (020) 8795-5050

Seating Capacity: 90,000 over three tiers –
    Lower Tier: 34,303 seats
    Middle Tier: 16,532 seats
    Upper Tier: 39,165 seats
Web site: www.wembleystadium.com

GENERAL INFORMATION

Car Parking: The stadium is a Public Transport Location and, as such, parking is only available for pre-accredited vehicles. Any spaces which are available must be pre-purchased from the following web site: www.csparking.com/stadium

Coach Travel: National Express operates 13 coach routes from 43 major towns and cities direct to the stadium for special events: www.nationalexpress.com/wembley

Rail & Tube Travel: Wembley Park station is on the Jubilee and Metropolitan tube lines; Wembley Stadium station is on the Bakerloo tube line and the Silver Link train line; Wembley Central station is on the Chiltern train line which runs from Marylebone Station

Local Bus Services: Services 18, 83, 92, 182 and 224 all travel to the stadium

DISABLED INFORMATION

Wheelchairs: 310 spaces for wheelchairs are available in total alongside 310 seats for helpers. A further 100 enhanced amenity seats are available for ambulant disabled visitors.

Disabled Toilets: Disabled toilets are available throughout the stadium.

ACCRINGTON STANLEY FC

Founded: 1876 (Reformed 1968)
Former Names: None
Nickname: 'Stanley' 'Reds'
Ground: The Fraser Eagle Stadium, Livingstone Road, Accrington, Lancashire   BB5 5BX
Record Attendance: 4,368 (3rd January 2004)
Pitch Size: 112 × 72 yards

Colours: Red shirts with White shorts
Telephone Nº: (01254) 356950
Fax Number: (01254) 356951
Ground Capacity: 5,050
Seating Capacity: 1,200
Web site: www.accringtonstanley.co.uk

GENERAL INFORMATION

Supporters Club: Malcolm Isherwood, c/o Club
Telephone Nº: –
Car Parking: 300 spaces available at the ground
Coach Parking: At the ground
Nearest Railway Station: Accrington (1 mile)
Nearest Bus Station: Accrington Town Centre (1 mile)
Club Shop: At the ground, at Oswaldtwistle Mills Shopping Village, at Fraser Eagle Worldchoice, Blackburn Road, Accrington and also through the club web site
Opening Times: Weekdays 9.00am – 5.00pm; Saturday matchdays 10.00am – 5.00pm
Telephone Nº: (01254) 356954
Police Telephone Nº: (01254) 382141

GROUND INFORMATION

Away Supporters' Entrances & Sections: Signposted on matchdays

ADMISSION INFO (2007/2008 PRICES)

Adult Standing: £13.00
Adult Seating: £15.00
Senior Citizen/Junior Standing: £8.00
Senior Citizen/Junior Seating: £10.00
Under-12s Standing: £4.00
Under-12s Seating: £5.00
Programme Price: £2.50

DISABLED INFORMATION

Wheelchairs: Specific areas around the ground
Helpers: Admitted
Prices: Concessionary prices are charged for the disabled. Helpers are admitted free of charge
Disabled Toilets: Available
Contact: (01254) 356950   Michael Schultz, Disabled Liaison Officer (Bookings are not necessary)

Travelling Supporters' Information:
Routes: Take the M6 to the M65 signposted for Blackburn/Burnley. Exit at Junction 7 and follow the sign for Padiham. Turn right at first traffic lights then right at next. Follow Whalley Road towards Accrington, go through lights at the Greyhound Inn. Turn left into Livingstone Road, 500 yards past traffic lights (signposted Accrington Stanley). The ground is signposted from Junction 7 of the M65 – follow the brown signs with the white football.

ARSENAL FC

Founded: 1886 (**Entered League**: 1893)
Former Names: Royal Arsenal (1886-1891) and
Woolwich Arsenal (1891-1914)
Nickname: 'Gunners'
Ground: Emirates Stadium, Drayton Park   N5
Ground Capacity: 60,432 (All seats)
Pitch Size: 110 × 71 yards
Record Attendance: 60,132 (3rd March 2007)

Colours: Red shirts with White sleeves, White shorts
Telephone Nº: (020) 7704-4000
Ticket Office: (020) 7704-4040
Fax Number: (020) 7704-4001
Recorded Ticket Information: (020) 7704-4242
Web Site: www.arsenal.com

GENERAL INFORMATION

Car Parking: None
Coach Parking: Visit the web site for further details
Nearest Railway Station: Finsbury Park and Highbury &
Islington
Nearest Tube Station: Arsenal (Piccadilly), Finsbury Park
and Highbury & Islington are all nearby
Club Shop: At the ground and at Finsbury Park Tube Station
Opening Times: Monday to Saturday 9.00am to 5.00pm;
Sundays 10.00am to 4.00pm
Telephone Nº: (020) 7704-4000
Police Telephone Nº: (020) 7263-9090

GROUND INFORMATION

Away Supporters' Entrances & Sections:
Green quadrant – follow colour coding system at the ground

ADMISSION INFO (2007/2008 PRICES)

Adult Seating: £32.00 – £94.00
Child Seating: £13.00 – £18.00 (In the Family Enclosure)
Senior Citizen Seating: £14.00 – £20.00 (Only in the
Family Enclosure)
Note: Prices vary depending on the category of the game.
Programme Price: £3.00

DISABLED INFORMATION

Wheelchairs: 250 spaces available in areas throughout the
ground. A similar number of places are available for the
ambulant disabled and visually impaired
Helpers: One helper admitted for each disabled supporter
Prices: Registered disabled supporters are admitted for half
the normal prices £16.00 – £47.00. Helpers are admitted free
Disabled Toilets: Many available throughout the ground
Free commentaries are available for the visually impaired
Contact: (020) 7704-4000 (Bookings are necessary)

Travelling Supporters' Information:
As the stadium is situated in a mainly residential area, only car owners with resident's permits will be allowed to park in the
designated on-street parking areas. Cars parked illegally will be towed away so use public transport whenever possible. The
nearest tube station is Arsenal (Piccadilly Line) which is 3 minutes walk from the ground with Finsbury Park (Victoria &
Piccadilly Lines) and Highbury & Islington about 10 minutes walk away.

ASTON VILLA FC

Founded: 1874 (**Entered League:** 1888)
Former Names: None
Nicknames: 'The Villans' 'Villa'
Ground: Villa Park, Trinity Road, Birmingham B6 6HE
Ground Capacity: 42,551 (All seats)
Record Attendance: 76,588 (2/3/46)
Pitch Size: 115 × 75 yards

Colours: Claret shirts with Blue sleeves, White shorts with Claret & Blue trim
Telephone N°: (0121) 327-2299
Fax Number: (0121) 322-2107
Consumer Sales: 0800 612-0970
Consumer Sales Fax Number: 0800 612-0977
Web Site: www.avfc.co.uk

GENERAL INFORMATION

Ground Tours: 0800 612-0970
Car Parking: Aston Villa Events Centre Car Park in Aston Hall Road.
Away Coach Parking: Opposite the ground
Nearest Railway Station: Witton or Aston (5 mins. walk)
Nearest Bus Station: Birmingham Centre
Club Shop: 'Villa Village' at the ground + also at Pavilions in Birmingham City Centre
Opening Times: Monday to Saturday 9.00am to 5.00pm. Also selected Sundays & Sunday Matchdays 10.00am to 2.00pm and 1 hour after the final whistle. City Centre shop open 9.30am to 6.00pm Monday to Saturday (Thursdays 6.30pm), 11.00am to 4.00pm on Sundays.
Telephone N°: 0800 612-0970
Police Telephone N°: (0845) 113-5000

GROUND INFORMATION

Away Supporters' Entrances & Sections:
North Stand – 'R' Block

ADMISSION INFO (2007/2008 PRICES)

Adult Seating: £15.00 – £35.00
Child Seating: £5.00 – £19.00
Programme Price: £2.50

DISABLED INFORMATION

Wheelchairs: 84 spaces in total in the Trinity Road Stand lower, 8 of which are for away supporters
Helpers: By letter or phone request – one per disabled fan
Prices: £15.00–£20.00 for each disabled supporter & helper
Disabled Toilets: Available in the Trinity Road Stand lower
Contact: 0800 612-0970 (Bookings are necessary)
E-mail contact: disability@avfc.co.uk

Travelling Supporters' Information: From all parts: Exit M6 at Junction 6 (Spaghetti Junction). Follow signs for Birmingham (NE). Take the 4th exit at the roundabout onto the A38 (M) signposted Aston. After ½ mile, turn right into Aston Hall Road.
Bus Services: Service 7 from Colmore Circus to Witton Square. Also some specials.

BARNET FC

Founded: 1888
Former Names: Barnet Alston FC
Nickname: 'The Bees'
Ground: Underhill Stadium, Barnet Lane, Barnet, Herts. EN5 2DN
Record Attendance: 11,026 (1952)
Pitch Size: 110 × 70 yards

Colours: Amber and Black shirts with Black shorts
Telephone Nº: (020) 8441-6932
Ticket Office: (020) 8449-6325
Fax Number: (020) 8447-0655
Ground Capacity: 5,345
Seating Capacity: 2,000 approximately
Web site: www.barnetfc.com

GENERAL INFORMATION

Supporters Club: K. Doe, c/o Club
Telephone Nº: –
Car Parking: Street Parking and High Barnet Underground Car Park
Coach Parking: By Police Direction
Nearest Railway Station: New Barnet (1½ miles)
Nearest Tube Station: High Barnet (Northern) (5 minutes walk)
Club Shop: 40 High Street, Barnet
Opening Times: Tuesday to Saturday 10.00am to 6.00pm
Telephone Nº: (020) 8440-0725
Police Telephone Nº: (020) 8200-2212

GROUND INFORMATION

Away Supporters' Entrances & Sections:
Entrances in Westcombe Drive for the North East Terrace

ADMISSION INFO (2007/2008 PRICES)

Adult Standing: £13.00 – £15.00
Adult Seating: £20.00 (£16.00 in the Family Stand)
Concessionary Seating: £12.00
Under-18/Senior Citizen Standing: £5 – £7 (Members)
Away Supporters: £15.00
Under-12 Members: Admitted free of charge
Programme Price: £2.50

DISABLED INFORMATION

Wheelchairs: 12 uncovered spaces in total for Home and Away fans on the North Terrace – Barnet Lane Entrance
Helpers: One helper admitted per wheelchair
Prices: Free of charge
Disabled Toilets: One available in the Social Club
Are Bookings Necessary: 24 hours notice required
Contact: (020) 8441-6932 ext. 215 (Beverly Bacon)

Travelling Supporters' Information:
Routes: The ground is situated off the Great North Road (A1000) at the foot of Barnet Hill near to the junction with Station Road (A110). Barnet Lane is on the west of the A1000 next to the Cricket Ground.

BARNSLEY FC

Founded: 1887 (**Entered League:** 1898)
Former Names: Barnsley St. Peter's
Nickname: 'Reds'
Ground: Oakwell Stadium, Barnsley   S71 1ET
Ground Capacity: 23,176 (All seats)
Record Attendance: 40,255 (15/2/36)
Pitch Size: 110 × 72 yards

Colours: Red shirts with White shorts and Red socks
Telephone Nº: (01226) 211211
Ticket Office: 0871 226-6777
Fax Number: (01226) 211444
Web Site: www.barnsleyfc.co.uk

GENERAL INFORMATION

Car Parking: Queen's Ground Car Park (adjacent)
Coach Parking: Queen's Ground Car Park
Nearest Railway Station: Barnsley Interchange (6 minutes walk)
Nearest Bus Station: Barnsley Interchange
Club Shop: At the Stadium
Opening Times: Monday to Friday 9.00am to 5.00pm. Saturdays 9.00am to 2.00pm. Saturday Matchdays open 9.00am to 3.00pm then 4.45pm to 5.15pm. Evening matchdays open 9.00am to 7.45pm
Telephone Nº: (01226) 211400
Police Telephone Nº: (0114) 220-2020

GROUND INFORMATION

Away Supporters' Entrances & Sections:
North Stand Turnstiles 42-51

ADMISSION INFO (2007/2008 PRICES)

Adult Seating: £20.00 – £22.00
Child Seating: £6.00 – £13.00
Concessionary Seating: £12.00 – £13.00
Programme Price: £3.00

DISABLED INFORMATION

Wheelchairs: A disabled stand provides accommodation to those in wheelchairs and blind supporters.
Helpers: Admitted depending on room available
Prices: £20.00 for the disabled but helpers are admitted free of charge
Disabled Toilets: Available in the Corner, North and Pontefract Road Stands
Commentaries are available for the blind
Contact: 0871 226-6777   (Bookings are necessary)

Travelling Supporters' Information: From All Parts: Exit the M1 at Junction 37 and follow the 'Barnsley FC/Football Ground' signs which lead to a large surface car park adjacent to the stadium (2 miles).

BIRMINGHAM CITY FC

Founded: 1875 (Entered League: 1892)
Former Names: Small Heath Alliance FC (1875-88);
Small Heath FC (1888-1905); Birmingham FC (1905-45)
Nickname: 'Blues'
Ground: St. Andrew's Stadium, Birmingham B9 4NH
Ground Capacity: 30,007 (All seats)
Record Attendance: 68,844 (11/2/39)

Pitch Size: 110 × 74 yards
Colours: Royal Blue Shirts with White trim, White
Shorts and Royal Blue socks
Telephone N°: 0844 557-1875
Ticket Office: 0844 557-1875 Option 2
Fax Number: 0844 557-1975
Web Site: www.bcfc.com

GENERAL INFORMATION

Car Parking: Street Parking + Birmingham Wheels (secure)
Coach Parking: Coventry Road
Nearest Railway Station: Birmingham New Street or
Birmingham Moor Street (20 minutes walk)
Nearest Bus Station: Digbeth
Club Shops: St. Andrew's Superstore and Birmingham
Pallasades
Opening Times: Monday to Saturday 9.30am to 5.30pm
and Sundays 10.00am to 4.00pm (Superstore only)
Telephone N°: (0121) 633-0444 (Pallasades) and
0844 557-1875 Option 4 (St. Andrew's Superstore)
Police Telephone N°: 0845 113-5000

GROUND INFORMATION

Away Supporters' Entrances & Sections:
Railway Stand End, Coventry Road

ADMISSION INFO (2007/2008 PRICES)

Adult Seating: £15.00 – £48.00
Child Seating: £5.00 – £25.00 (Family tickets are available)
Note: Prices vary depending on the match category
Programme Price: £3.00

DISABLED INFORMATION

Wheelchairs: Spaces available in the Spion Kop Stand,
Family Stand, Railway Stand and Tilton Road Stand
Helpers: One assistant admitted for each disabled fan
Prices: £20.00 for each disabled fan plus an assistant
Disabled Toilets: Available in the Spion Kop Stand, Family
Stand, Railway Stand and Tilton Road Stand
Contact: 0844 557-1875 Option 2 (Bookings are necessary)

Travelling Supporters' Information: From All Parts: Exit M6 at Junction 6 and take the A38 (M) (Aston Expressway). Leave
at 2nd exit then take first exit at roundabout along the Dartmouth Middleway. After 1¼ miles turn left into St. Andrew's Street.
Bus Services: Services 96 & 97 from Birmingham; Services 98 & 99 from Digbeth

BLACKBURN ROVERS FC

Founded: 1875 (**Entered League**: 1888)
Nickname: 'Rovers' 'Blues & Whites'
Ground: Ewood Park, Blackburn,
Lancashire   BB2 4JF
Pitch Size: 115 × 72 yards
Ground Capacity: 31,154 (All seats)
Record Attendance: 62,255 vs Bolton (2/3/1929)

Colours: Blue and White halved shirts, White shorts
Telephone Nº: 08701 113232
Ticket Office: 08701 123456
Fax Number: (01254) 671042
Web Site: www.rovers.co.uk

GENERAL INFORMATION

Car Parking: 800 spaces available at the ground
Coach Parking: At the ground
Nearest Railway Station: Blackburn Central (1½ miles)
Nearest Bus Station: Blackburn Central (1½ miles)
Club Shop: At the ground
Opening Times: Monday to Saturday 9.00am – 5.00pm;
Saturday Matchdays 9.00am–3.00pm and 4.45pm–5.30pm;
Sundays 12.00pm – 3.00pm
Telephone Nº: (01254) 695348
Police Telephone Nº: (01254) 51212

GROUND INFORMATION

Away Supporters' Entrances & Sections: Darwen End

ADMISSION INFO (2007/2008 PRICES)

Adult Seating: £15.00 – £39.00
Child Seating: £7.00 – £16.00
Concessions Seating: £15.00 – £39.00
Note: Prices vary depending on the category of the game
Programme Price: £3.00

DISABLED INFORMATION

Wheelchairs: 262 spaces in total for Home and Away fans
Helpers: One helper admitted per disabled fan. Please note
that applications for helpers tickets must be made in advance
Prices: 70% off usual prices for the disabled. Free for helpers
Disabled Toilets: 14 purpose-built ground level toilets
Commentaries available by arrangement for up to 6 people
Contact: 08701 113232   (Bookings are necessary)

Travelling Supporters' Information: Routes: Supporters travelling Northbound on the M6: Exit the M6 at Junction 29,
follow the M65 and exit at Junction 4 for Ewood Park. The ground is ¾ mile from Junction 4 – please look for parking areas to
avoid congestion around the ground; Supporters travelling Northbound on the M61: Exit the M61 at Junction 9, join the M65
and exit at Junction 4 (then as above); Supporters travelling Southbound on the M6: Exit the M6 at Junction 30, follow the
M61 and exit at Junction 9 onto the M65. Exit the M65 at Junction 4 for the ground; Supporters from the Yorkshire Area either
on the B6234, the A56 Haslingden by-pass or the A59 Skipton Road – please follow signs for Ewood Park (follow Preston M65
and exit at Junction 4).

BLACKPOOL FC

Founded: 1887 (**Entered League**: 1896)
Former Name: Merged with Blackpool St. Johns (1887)
Nickname: 'Seasiders' or 'Tangerines'
Ground: Bloomfield Road, Blackpool, FY1 6JJ
Ground Capacity: 16,000 seats (When development is completed)
Record Attendance: 38,098 (17th September 1955)

Pitch Size: 110 × 74 yards
Colours: Tangerine shirts with White shorts
Telephone Nº: (0870) 443-1953
Ticket Office: (0870) 443-1953
Fax Number: (01253) 405011
Web Site: www.blackpoolfc.co.uk

GENERAL INFORMATION

Car Parking: 3,000 spaces at the ground and street parking
Coach Parking: Available at the ground
Nearest Railway Station: Blackpool South (5 mins. walk)
Nearest Bus Station: Talbot Road (2 miles)
Club Shop: At the ground
Opening Times: Daily from 9.00am to 5.15pm
Telephone Nº: (0870) 443-1953

GROUND INFORMATION

Away Supporters' Entrances & Sections:
East Stand (Uncovered)

ADMISSION INFO (2007/2008 PRICES)

Adult Seating: £18.00 – £21.50
Under-16s Seating: £9.00 – £12.50
Senior Citizen Seating: £13.00 – £17.00
Note: Discounted prices are available for advance purchases
Programme Price: £2.50

DISABLED INFORMATION

Wheelchairs: Over 50 spaces in total for home and away fans in the new North and West Stands
Helpers: One helper admitted per disabled fan
Prices: £8.50 for the Disabled. £8.50 for Helpers
Disabled Toilets: Available
Contact: (0870) 443-1953 (Bookings are necessary)

Travelling Supporters' Information: From All Parts: Exit M6 at Junction 32 onto the M55. Follow signs for the main car parks along the new 'spine' road to the car parks at the side of the ground.

BOLTON WANDERERS FC

Founded: 1874 (**Entered League:** 1888)
Former Names: Christchurch FC (1874-1877)
Nickname: 'Trotters'
Ground: Reebok Stadium, Burnden Way, Lostock, Bolton, Lancashire BL6 6JW
Ground Capacity: 27,879 (All seats)
Pitch Size: 110 × 70 yards

Record Attendance: 27,409
Colours: White shirts and shorts
Telephone Nº: (01204) 673673
Ticket Office: (0871) 871-2932
Fax Number: (0871) 871-8183
Web Site: www.bwfc.co.uk

GENERAL INFORMATION

Car Parking: 2,800 spaces available at the ground
Coach Parking: Available at the ground
Nearest Railway Station: Horwich Parkway (600 yards)
Nearest Bus Station: Moor Lane, Bolton
Club Shop: At the ground
Opening Times: Daily from 9.30am to 5.30pm
Telephone Nº: (01204) 673650
Police Telephone Nº: (01204) 522466

GROUND INFORMATION

Away Supporters' Entrances & Sections:
South Stand entrances and accommodation

ADMISSION INFO (2006/2007 PRICES)

Adult Seating: £21.00 – £39.00
Child Seating: £10.00 – £21.00
Senior Citizen Seating: £16.00 – £28.00
Note: Special family tickets are also available
Programme Price: £2.50

DISABLED INFORMATION

Wheelchairs: 32 spaces available for visiting fans, 72 spaces for home fans
Helpers: One helper admitted per disabled fan
Prices: Free for wheelchair users. Helpers normal prices
Disabled Toilets: Yes
Contact: (01204) 673673 (Bookings are necessary)

Travelling Supporters' Information:
From All Parts: Exit the M61 at Junction 6 and the ground is clearly visible ¼ mile away.

AFC BOURNEMOUTH

Founded: 1899 (**Entered League**: 1923)
Former Names: Boscombe FC (1899-1923);
Bournemouth & Boscombe Athletic FC (1923-1972)
Nickname: 'Cherries'
Ground: The Fitness First Stadium at Dean Court,
Bournemouth, Dorset   BH7 7AF
Ground Capacity: 10,375 (All seats)

Record Attendance: 9,359 (6th May 2006)
Pitch Size: 115 × 74 yards
Colours: Red shirts with Black shorts
Telephone N°: (01202) 726300
Ticket Office: (01202) 726303
Fax Number: (01202) 726301
Web Site: www.afcb.co.uk

GENERAL INFORMATION

Car Parking: Car Park for 1,500 cars behind Main Stand
Coach Parking: Kings Park (nearby)
Nearest Railway Station: Bournemouth Central (1½ miles)
Nearest Bus Station: Holdenhurst Road, Bournemouth
Club Shop: At the ground
Opening Times: Weekdays 9.00am to 5.00pm;
Saturday Matchdays 9.00am to kick-off
Telephone N°: (01202) 726325
Police Telephone N°: (01202) 552099

GROUND INFORMATION

Away Supporters' Entrances & Sections:
East Stand turnstiles 'F' 14-16 for East Stand accommodation
(Away ticket office is adjacent)

ADMISSION INFO (2007/2008 PRICES)

Adult Seating: £14.00 – £26.50
Child Seating: £7.00 – £17.50
Concessionary Seating: £7.00 – £17.50
Note: Prices vary depending on the category of the game
Programme Price: £3.00

DISABLED INFORMATION

Wheelchairs: 100 spaces in total for Home and Away fans
in various stands
Helpers: One helper admitted per disabled fan
Prices: Free of charge for both the disabled and helpers
Disabled Toilets: Available in all Stands
Contact: (07803) 090047   (Bookings are necessary)

Travelling Supporters' Information: Routes: From the North & East: Take the A338 into Bournemouth and turn left at 'Kings Park' turning. After the slip road go straight forward at the mini-roundabout into Kings Park Drive – a car park is 500 yards on the left and the ground is nearby; From the West: Use the A3049, turning right at Wallisdown Roundabout to Talbot Roundabout. Take the first exit at Talbot Roundabout (over Wessex Way), then left at the mini-roundabout. Go straight on at the traffic lights then right at the mini-roundabout into Kings Park for the ground.

BRADFORD CITY FC

Founded: 1903 (**Entered League:** 1903)
Nickname: 'Bantams'
Ground: Intersonic Stadium, Valley Parade, Bradford BD8 7DY
Ground Capacity: 25,134 (All seats)
Record Attendance: 39,146 (11/3/11)
Pitch Size: 113 × 70 yards

Colours: Claret and Amber shirts and Black shorts
Telephone N°: 0870 822-0000
Ticket Office: 0870 822-1911
Fax Number: (01274) 773356
Marketing Department: 0870 822-0100
Web Site: www.bradfordcityfc.co.uk

GENERAL INFORMATION

Car Parking: Street Parking and Car Parks (£3.00 charge)
Coach Parking: By Police direction
Nearest Railway Station: Bradford Foster Square
Nearest Bus Station: Bradford Interchange (1 mile)
Club Shop: At the ground
Opening Times: Monday to Friday 9.00am to 5.00pm, Saturday 9.00am to 3.00pm
Telephone N°: 0870 822-7700
Police Telephone N°: (01274) 723422

GROUND INFORMATION

Away Supporters' Entrances & Sections:
TL Dallas Stand entrances and accommodation

ADMISSION INFO (2007/2008 PRICES)

Adult Seating: £20.00
Child Seating: £12.00
Note: Special concessions are available in the Family Stand
Programme Price: £2.50

DISABLED INFORMATION

Wheelchairs: 100 spaces available in total for Home and Away fans in the disabled area, 'A' Block of Sunwin Stand and also in the Carlsberg Stand & East Stand
Helpers: One helper admitted per disabled fan
Prices: Half-price for disabled fans and helpers
Disabled Toilets: Available behind the disabled area
Contact: 0870 822-1911 (Bookings are necessary)

Travelling Supporters' Information: Routes: Exit the M62 at Junction 26 and take the M606 towards Bradford. At the end of the motorway get in the middle lane and follow signs for Bradford (West) into Rooley Lane (signs for the Airport). A McDonalds is now on your left. Turn left into Wakefield Road at the roundabout and stay in the middle lane. Continue straight on over two roundabouts (signs to Shipley and Skipton) onto Shipley Airedale Road which then becomes Canal Road. Just after Tesco on the left, turn left into Station Road and left again into Queens Road. Go up the hill to the third set of traffic lights and turn left into Manningham Lane. After the Gulf petrol station on the left, turn first left into Valley Parade for the Stadium.

BRENTFORD FC

Founded: 1889 (**Entered League:** 1920)
Nickname: 'The Bees'
Ground: Griffin Park, Braemar Road, Brentford, Middlesex TW8 0NT
Ground Capacity: 12,800
Seating Capacity: 10,200
Record Attendance: 39,626 (1938)

Pitch Size: 110 × 74 yards
Colours: Red & White striped shirts with Black shorts
Telephone N°: 0845 3456-442
Ticket Office: 0845 3456-442
Fax Number: (020) 8568-9940
Web Site: www.brentfordfc.co.uk

GENERAL INFORMATION

Car Parking: Street Parking
Coach Parking: Layton Road Car Park
Nearest Railway Station: Brentford (½ mile)
Nearest Tube Station: South Ealing (Piccadilly) (1 mile)
Club Shop: At the ground in Braemar Road
Opening Times: Weekdays & matchdays 9.00am–5.00pm.
Telephone N°: 0845 3456-442
Police Telephone N°: (020) 8569-9728

GROUND INFORMATION

Away Supporters' Entrances & Sections:
Braemar Road and Ealing Road – entrance via Braemar Road

ADMISSION INFO (2007/2008 PRICES)

Adult Standing: £18.00
Adult Seating: £19.00 or £20.00
Juniors Standing/Seating: £5.00
Students/Senior Citizen Standing: £12.00
Students/Senior Citizen Seating: £13.00 or £14.00
Programme Price: £2.50

DISABLED INFORMATION

Wheelchairs: 10 spaces for Home fans, 2 spaces for Away fans in the disabled section, Braemar Road
Helpers: One helper admitted per disabled fan
Prices: Normal prices for the disabled. Free for helpers
Disabled Toilets: Available in the disabled section
Commentaries are available for the blind
Contact: 0845 3456-442 (Bookings are necessary)

Travelling Supporters' Information: Routes: From the North: Take the A406 North Circular (from the M1/A1) to the Chiswick Roundabout and then along the Great West Road and turn left at the third set of traffic lights into Ealing Road for the ground; From the East: Take the A406 to the Chiswick Roundabout, then as North; From the West: Exit M4 at Junction 2 – down to the Chiswick Roundabout, then as North; From the South: Use the A3, M3, A240 or A316 to Kew Road, continue along over Kew Bridge, turn left at the traffic lights, then right at the next traffic lights into Ealing Road.

BRIGHTON & HOVE ALBION FC

Founded: 1901 (**Entered League:** 1920)
Nickname: 'Seagulls'
Office: North West Suite, 8th Floor, Tower Point, 44 North Road, Brighton BN1 1YR
Ground: Withdean Stadium, Tongdean Lane, off London Road, Brighton BN1 5JD
Ground Capacity: 8,850 (All seats)
Pitch Size: 110 × 70 yards

Record Attendance: 7,999 (8th April 2006)
Colours: Blue & White striped shirts, White shorts
Telephone Nº: (01273) 695400
Ticket Office: (01273) 776992
Ticket Office Address: 5 Queen's Road, Brighton
Fax Number: (01273) 648179
Web Site: www.seagulls.co.uk

GENERAL INFORMATION
Car Parking: No parking near the stadium – take park & ride buses or walk
Coach Parking: By Police direction
Nearest Railway Station: Preston Park (10 minutes walk)
Nearest Bus Station: Brighton
Club Shop: 5/6 Queen's Road, Brighton
Opening Times: Monday–Saturday 9.30am-5.30pm (shop closes at 5.00pm on Home matchdays)
Telephone Nº: (01273) 776969

GROUND INFORMATION
Away Supporters' Entrances & Sections:
West Stand (Block X)

ADMISSION INFO (2007/2008 PRICES)
Adult Seating: £23.50 – £27.00
Child Seating: £14.00 – £17.00
Senior Citizen Seating: £15.50 – £18.50
Note: Advanced booking only – no tickets are available at the ground (matches are always all-ticket).
Programme Price: £3.00

DISABLED INFORMATION
Wheelchairs: Limited spaces for Home fans in the disabled section, South Stand and Away fans in the West Stand
Helpers: One helper admitted per disabled person
Prices: £16.50 for the disabled. Helpers are admitted free
Disabled Toilets: Yes
Contact: (01273) 776992 (Bookings are necessary)

Travelling Supporters' Information: Routes: From the North: Take the M23 then the A23 to Brighton. The ground is situated in Tongdean Lane which is directly off the A23 (London Road) just after Peacock Lane but, as no parking is available around the ground, a park and ride scheme will operate from Mill Road which is close to the junction of the A23 and the A27; From the East and West: Take the A27 into Brighton to the A23 then as above.

BRISTOL CITY FC

Founded: 1894 (**Entered League**: 1901)
Former Name: Bristol South End FC (1894-1897)
Nickname: 'The Robins'
Ground: Ashton Gate Stadium, Bristol BS3 2EJ
Ground Capacity: 21,497 (All seats)
Pitch Size: 115 × 75 yards
Record Attendance: 43,335 (16/2/35)

Colours: Red shirts with Red shorts
Telephone Nº: 0870 112-1897
Ticket Hotline: 0870 112-1897
Fax Number: (0117) 963-0700
Web Site: www.bcfc.co.uk

GENERAL INFORMATION

Car Parking: Street parking
Coach Parking: Ashton Vale Trading Estate (contact Police)
Nearest Railway Station: Bristol Temple Meads (1½ miles)
Nearest Bus Station: Bristol City Centre
Club Shop: At the ground
Opening Times: Weekdays 8.30am to 5.00pm and Saturdays 9.00am to 12.00pm
Telephone Nº: 0870 112-1897
Police Telephone Nº: (0117) 927-7777

GROUND INFORMATION

Away Supporters' Entrances & Sections:
Wedlock Stand

ADMISSION INFO (2007/2008 PRICES)

Adult Seating: £25.00 – £30.00
Under-16s Seating: £15.00 – £21.00
Concessionary Seating: £20.00 – £24.00
Note: Discounts are available for advance bookings
Programme Price: £3.00

DISABLED INFORMATION

Wheelchairs: Limited number accommodated at pitchside – please apply early
Helpers: One helper admitted per disabled fan
Prices: Normal prices for the disabled. Free for helpers
Disabled Toilets: 2 available
Commentaries are available for the blind (contact the club for further information)
Contact: 0870 112-1897 (Bookings are necessary)

Travelling Supporters' Information: Routes: From the North & West: Exit the M5 at Junction 16, take the A38 to Bristol City Centre and follow the A38 Taunton signs. Cross the swing bridge after 1¼ miles and bear left into Winterstoke Road for the ground; From the East: Take the M4 then M32 and follow signs for the City Centre. Then as for North and West; From the South: Exit the M5 at Junction 18 and follow Taunton signs over the swing bridge (then as above).
Bus Services: Services 27A and 28A from the Railway Station.

BRISTOL ROVERS FC

In early 2008 the club expect to begin re-development of the Memorial Stadium at which stage they are expected to groundshare with Cheltenham Town. Please contact the club for further information.

Founded: 1883 (**Entered League:** 1920)
Former Names: Black Arabs FC (1883-84);
Eastville Rovers FC (1884-96);
Bristol Eastville Rovers FC (1896-97)
Nickname: 'Pirates' 'Rovers' 'Gas'
Ground: Memorial Stadium, Filton Avenue, Horfield,
Bristol BS7 0BF
Pitch Size: 110 × 71 yards

Ground Capacity: 11,917
Seating Capacity: 3,000
Record Attendance: 11,433 (2000)
Colours: Blue & White quartered shirts, White shorts
Telephone Nº: (0117) 909-6648
Fax Number: (0117) 909-8848
Web Site: www.bristolrovers.co.uk

GENERAL INFORMATION
Car Parking: Approximately 300 spaces at ground (pre-booked only) and street parking
Coach Parking: At the ground
Nearest Railway Station: Temple Meads (2 miles)
Nearest Bus Station: Bristol City Centre
Club Shop: 199 Two Mile Hill Road, Kingswood and also at Pirate Leisure, Memorial Stadium, Filton Avenue
Opening Times: Supporters' Club: Weekdays 9.00am to 5.00pm and Saturdays 9.00am to 1.00pm; Pirate Leisure: Weekdays 9.00am to 5.00pm, Saturdays 9.00am to 1.00pm (Home matchdays 9.00am – 2.45pm then 4.45pm – 5.15pm)
Telephone Nº: (0117) 961-1772 + (0117) 909-6648

GROUND INFORMATION
Away Supporters' Entrances & Sections:
Entrance to Centenary Terrace & South Stand via Filton Avenue

ADMISSION INFO (2007/2008 PRICES)
Adult Standing: £17.00–£19.00
Adult Seating: £20.00 – £25.00
Child Standing: £7.00 – £11.00
Child Seating: £10.00 – £19.50
Discounts are available if tickets are bought before matchdays
Programme Price: £2.50

DISABLED INFORMATION
Wheelchairs: Unspecified number accommodated in front of the Mead Civil Engineering Stand and DAS Stand
Helpers: One helper admitted per disabled person
Prices: £10.00 for wheelchair and ambulant disabled. Helpers are admitted free of charge
Disabled Toilets: In the Mead Stand and DAS Stand
Contact: (0117) 909-6648 (Bookings are necessary)

Travelling Supporters' Information: Routes: From All Parts: Exit the M32 at Junction 2 then take the exit at the roundabout (signposted Horfield) into Muller Road. Continue for approximately 1½ miles passing straight across 3 sets of traffic lights. At the 6th set of traffic lights turn left into Filton Avenue and the ground is immediately on the left.

BURNLEY FC

Founded: 1882 (**Entered League**: 1888)
Former Name: Burnley Rovers FC
Nickname: 'Clarets'
Ground: Turf Moor, Harry Potts Way, Burnley, Lancashire   BB10 4BX
Ground Capacity: 22,610 (All seats)
Record Attendance: 54,775 (23/2/24)

Pitch Size: 112 × 70 yards
Colours: Claret and Blue shirts with Claret shorts
Telephone N°: (0870) 443-1882
Ticket Office: (0870) 443-1914
Fax Number: (01282) 700014
Web Site: www.burnleyfc.com

GENERAL INFORMATION

Car Parking: Ormerod Road, adjacent to the Fire Station (2 minutes walk) and Fulledge Recreation Ground (2 mins. walk)
Coach Parking: By Police direction
Nearest Railway Station: Burnley Central (1½ miles)
Nearest Bus Station: Burnley (5 minutes walk)
Club Shop: At the ground
Opening Times: Monday to Friday 9.00am – 5.00pm; Saturdays 9.00am – 5.00pm
Telephone N°: (0870) 443-1882
Police Telephone N°: (01282) 425001

GROUND INFORMATION

Away Supporters' Entrances & Sections:
Cricket Field Stand

ADMISSION INFO (2007/2008 PRICES)

Adult Seating: £19.00 – £22.00
Child Seating: £9.00 – £11.00
Programme Price: £2.50

DISABLED INFORMATION

Wheelchairs: Three designated wheelchair areas
Helpers: One helper admitted for each wheelchair user
Prices: £18.00 for each disabled fan plus one helper
Disabled Toilets: Available
Commentaries are available via headsets
Non-wheelchair disabled, please phone for further details
Contact: (0870) 443-1914   (Bookings are necessary)

Travelling Supporters' Information: Routes: From the North: Follow the A682 to the Town Centre and take first exit at roundabout (Gala Club) into Yorkshire Street. Follow through traffic signals into Harry Potts Way; From the East: Follow the A646 to the A671 then along Todmorden Road towards the Town Centre. At the traffic signals (crossroads) turn right into Harry Potts Way; From the West & South: Exit the M6 at Junction 29 onto the M65. Exit the M65 at Junction 10 and follow signs for Burnley Football Club. At the roundabout in the town centre take the third exit into Yorkshire Street. Then as from the North.

BURY FC

Founded: 1885 (**Entered League:** 1894)
Nickname: 'Shakers'
Ground: Gigg Lane, Bury, Lancashire BL9 9HR
Ground Capacity: 11,669 (All seats)
Pitch Size: 112 × 72 yards
Record Attendance: 35,000 (9/1/60)

Colours: White shirts, Royal Blue shorts
Telephone Nº: (0161) 764-4881
Ticket Office: (0161) 764-4881
General Fax Number: (0161) 764-5521
Commercial Dept. Fax Number: (0161) 763-3103
Web Site: www.buryfc.co.uk

GENERAL INFORMATION
Car Parking: Street Parking
Coach Parking: By Police direction
Nearest Railway Station: Bury Interchange (1 mile)
Nearest Bus Station: Bury Interchange
Club Shop: At the ground
Opening Times: Monday to Friday and Saturday matchdays 9.00am to 5.00pm
Telephone Nº: (0161) 762-0528
Police Telephone Nº: (0161) 872-5050

GROUND INFORMATION
Away Supporters' Entrances & Sections:
Gigg Lane entrance for the East Stand

ADMISSION INFO (2007/2008 PRICES)
Adult Seating: £14.00 – £16.00
Child/Senior Citizen Seating: £7.00 (Over-62s qualify)
Note: Family concessions are also available
Programme Price: £2.50

DISABLED INFORMATION
Wheelchairs: Spaces for 26 wheelchairs in disabled section (home area) and a further 25 spaces in the Away Supporters' Section
Helpers: One helper admitted per wheelchair
Prices: £7.00 for the disabled. Free of charge for helpers
Disabled Toilets: Available in disabled section
A Radio Commentary is available in the Press Box for the Registered Blind
Contact: (0161) 764-4881 (Bookings are not necessary)

Travelling Supporters' Information: Routes: From the North: Exit the M66 at Junction 2, take Bury Road (A58) for ½ mile, then turn left into Heywood Street and follow this into Parkhills Road until its end, turn left into Manchester Road (A56) and then left again into Gigg Lane. From the South, East and West: Exit the M60 at Junction 17, take Bury Road (A56) for 3 miles and then turn right into Gigg Lane.

CARDIFF CITY FC

Founded: 1899 **(Entered League:** 1920)
Former Names: Riverside FC (1899-1910)
Nickname: 'Bluebirds'
Ground: Ninian Park, Sloper Road, Cardiff CF11 8SX
Record Attendance: 62,634 (17/10/59)
Ground Capacity: 20,324
Seating Capacity: 12,891
Pitch Size: 110 × 75 yards

Colours: Royal Blue shirts with White shorts
Telephone Nº: (029) 2022-1001
Home Support Ticket Office: (0845) 345-1400
Away Support Ticket Office: (0845) 345-1405
Fax Number: (029) 2034-1148
Web Site: www.cardiffcityfc.co.uk

GENERAL INFORMATION

Car Parking: Leckwith Stadium car park and Street Parking
Coach Parking: Leckwith Stadium car park (adjacent)
Nearest Railway Station: Cardiff Central (1 mile)
Nearest Bus Station: Cardiff Central
Club Shop: At the ground
Opening Times: Weekdays from 9.00am to 5.00pm and Matchdays 10.00am to 3.00pm
Telephone Nº: (0845) 345-1485
Postal Sales: Yes (Internet Sales also accepted)
Police Telephone Nº: (029) 2022-2111

GROUND INFORMATION

Away Supporters' Entrances & Sections:
Grange End Visitors section entrances and accommodation (both standing and seating). Use turnstiles at Entrance F

ADMISSION INFO (2007/2008 PRICES)

Adult Standing: £16.00 – £24.00
Adult Seating: £18.00 – £30.00
Child Standing: £10.00 – £15.00
Child Seating: £5.00 – £22.00
Note: Tickets are cheaper if purchased before the matchday
Programme Price: £3.00

DISABLED INFORMATION

Wheelchairs: 28 spaces available for Home fans, 6 spaces for Away fans in the disabled section, Canton End Family Enclosure
Helpers: One helper admitted per disabled fan
Prices: Disabled children – £5.00; Disabled adults – £18.00; Disabled OAPs – £10.00; Helpers admitted free of charge
Disabled Toilets: Yes
Contact: (0845) 345-1405 (Away fans tickets are normally sold in advance but may be available on the day)

Travelling Supporters' Information:
Routes: From All Parts: Exit M4 at Junction 33 and follow Penarth (A4232) signs. After 6 miles, take the B4267 to Ninian Park.

CARLISLE UNITED FC

Founded: 1903 (**Entered League:** 1928)
Former Names: Formed with the amalgamation of Shaddongate United FC and Carlisle Red Rose FC
Nickname: 'Cumbrians' 'Blues'
Ground: Brunton Park Stadium, Warwick Road, Carlisle   CA1 1LL
Ground Capacity: 16,982
Seating Capacity: 6,380

Record Attendance: 27,500 (5/1/57)
Pitch Size: 112 × 74 yards
Colours: Royal Blue and White shirts and shorts
Telephone Nº: (01228) 526237
Ticket Office: (01228) 526237 Option 1
Fax Number: (01228) 554141
Web Site: www.carlisleunited.co.uk

GENERAL INFORMATION
Car Parking: Rear of Ground via St. Aidans Road
Coach Parking: St. Aidans Road Car Park
Nearest Railway Station: Carlisle Citadel (1 mile)
Nearest Bus Station: Lowther Street, Carlisle
Club Shop: At the ground and in the City Centre
Opening Times: Monday to Saturday 10.00am – 5.30pm
Telephone Nº: (01228) 554138
Police Telephone Nº: (01228) 528191

GROUND INFORMATION
Away Supporters' Entrances & Sections:
Turnstiles 14-16 for the Petteril End

ADMISSION INFO (2007/2008 PRICES)
Adult Standing: £16.00
Adult Seating: £20.00
Ages 11-17 Standing: £9.00
Ages 11-17 Seating: £10.00
Under-11s Standing: £3.00   **Under-11s Seating:** £4.00
Senior Citizen Standing: £12.00
Senior Citizen Seating: £14.00
Note: Adult tickets are cheaper prior to the matchday
Programme Price: £2.50

DISABLED INFORMATION
Wheelchairs: 17 spaces for wheelchairs in the disabled section, in front of the New East Stand
Helpers: One helper admitted per disabled fan
Prices: Wheelchair disabled admitted for £1.00. Helpers are admitted free of charge
Disabled Toilets: Yes
Contact: (01228) 526237   (Bookings are recommended)

Travelling Supporters' Information:
Routes: From the North, South and East: Exit the M6 at Junction 43 and follow signs for Carlisle (A69) into Warwick Road for the ground; From the West: Take the A69 straight into Warwick Road.

CHARLTON ATHLETIC FC

Founded: 1905 (**Entered League**: 1921)
Nickname: 'Addicks'
Ground: The Valley, Floyd Road, Charlton, London, SE7 8BL
Ground Capacity: 27,111 (All seats)
Record Attendance: 75,031 (12/2/38)
Pitch Size: 111 × 73 yards

Colours: Red shirts with White shorts
Telephone No: (020) 8333-4000
Ticket Office: 0871 226-1905
Fax Number: (020) 8333-4001
Web Site: www.cafc.co.uk

GENERAL INFORMATION

Car Parking: Street Parking
Coach Parking: By Police direction
Nearest Railway Station: Charlton (2 minutes walk)
Nearest Bus Station: At Charlton Railway Station as above
Club Shop: At the ground
Opening Times: Weekdays 10.00am – 6.00pm
Non-Match Saturdays 10.00am – 2.00pm
Telephone No: (020) 8333-4035
Police Telephone No: (020) 8853-8212

GROUND INFORMATION

Away Supporters' Entrances & Sections:
Valley Grove/Jimmy Seed Stand

ADMISSION INFO (2007/2008 PRICES)

Adult Seating: £20.00 – £45.00
Child Seating: £5.00 – £25.00
Concessions Seating: £10.00 – £25.00
Programme Price: £3.00

DISABLED INFORMATION

Wheelchairs: 96 spaces available for Home fans in the West and East Stands. 7 spaces available for Away fans in the South (Jimmy Seed) Stand
Helpers: One helper admitted per disabled fan
Prices: Helpers are admitted free of charge. Wheelchair disabled pay concessionary prices
Disabled Toilets: Available in West and East Stands
Commentaries are available – please ring for details
Contact: 0871 226-1905 (Bookings are necessary)

Travelling Supporters' Information:
Routes: From All Parts: Exit the M25 at Junction 2 (A2 London-bound) and follow until the road becomes the A102(M). Take the exit marked Woolwich Ferry and turn right along the A206 Woolwich Road. After approximately 1 mile do a U-turn at the roundabout back along Woolwich Road. At the traffic lights turn left into Charlton Church Lane and Floyd Road is the 2nd left.

CHELSEA FC

Founded: 1905 (**Entered League:** 1905)
Nickname: 'Blues'
Ground: Stamford Bridge, Fulham Road, London, SW6 1HS
Ground Capacity: 42,055 (All seats)
Record Attendance: 82,905 (12/10/35)
Pitch Size: 113 × 74 yards

Colours: Blue shirts and shorts
Telephone Nº: 0871 984-1955 (UK callers); +44 20-7915-2900 (International callers)
Fax Number: (020) 7381-4831
Web Site: www.chelseafc.com

GENERAL INFORMATION

Car Parking: Pre-booked underground car park at ground
Coach Parking: By Police direction
Nearest Tube Station: Fulham Broadway (District)
Club Shop: Chelsea Megastore – at the ground
Opening Times: Monday to Saturday 10.00am – 6.00pm; Sundays 10.00am–4.00pm; Bank Holidays 11.00am – 5.00pm Stadium tours are also available
Telephone Nº: 0871 231-0005
Police Telephone Nº: (020) 7385-1212

GROUND INFORMATION

Away Supporters' Entrances & Sections:
Shed End

ADMISSION INFO (2007/2008 PRICES)

Adult Seating: £35.00 – £60.00
Child Seating: £15.00 (Members only)
Senior Citizen Seating: £15.00 (Members only)
Note: Discounted prices are available to members and also in the Family Stand
Programme Price: £3.00

DISABLED INFORMATION

Disabled Seating: 290 spaces (including helpers) in total for Home and Away fans in the disabled area
Helpers: One helper admitted per disabled person
Prices: Free of charge for the disabled
Disabled Toilets: Available in the East Stand Concourse, West Stand and also in the Matthew Harding Stand
Free commentaries for blind supporters are available
Contact: (020) 7915-1950 (Bookings are necessary)

Travelling Supporters' Information:
Routes: From the North & East: Follow Central London signs from the A1/M1 to Hyde Park Corner, then signs for Guildford (A3) to Knightsbridge (A4). After 1 mile turn left into Fulham Road; From the South: Take the A13 or A24 then the A219 to cross Putney Bridge and follow signs for 'West End' (A304) to join the A308 into Fulham Road; From the West: Take the M4 then A4 to Central London, then follow signs to Westminster (A3220). After ¾ mile, turn right at crossroads into Fulham Road.

CHELTENHAM TOWN FC

Founded: 1892 (**Entered League**: 1999)
Nickname: 'Robins'
Ground: Whaddon Road, Cheltenham,
Gloucestershire   GL52 5NA
Ground Capacity: 7,136
Seating Capacity: 4,054
Record Attendance: 8,326 (1956)

Pitch Size: 110 × 72 yards
Colours: Red and White shirts with White shorts
Telephone Nº: (01242) 573558
Fax Number: (01242) 224675
Web Site: www.ctfc.com

GENERAL INFORMATION

Car Parking: No parking is available at the ground.
A complementary Park & Ride scheme runs from Cheltenham
Race Course
Coach Parking: Please phone for details
Nearest Railway Station: Cheltenham Spa (2½ miles)
Nearest Bus Station: Cheltenham Royal Well
Club Shop: At the ground
Opening Times: Weekdays & Matchdays 10.00am–2.45pm.
Telephone Nº: (01242) 573558
Police Telephone Nº: (01242) 528282

GROUND INFORMATION

Away Supporters' Entrances & Sections:
Carlsberg Stand (entrance from Whaddon Road)

ADMISSION INFO (2007/2008 PRICES)

Adult Standing: £13.00
Adult Seating: £17.00 or £18.00
Child Standing: £5.00 (under-16s)
Child Seating: £7.00 (under-16s)
Concessionary Standing: £9.00
Concessionary Seating: £11.00 or £12.00
Programme Price: £2.50

DISABLED INFORMATION

Wheelchairs: Accommodated in front of the UCAS Stand
(use the main entrance) and in the In 2 Print Stand
Helpers: Admitted free of charge
Prices: Concessionary prices are charged
Disabled Toilets: Available in the In 2 Print Stand, adjacent
to the UCAS Stand and in the Social Club
Contact: (01242) 573558   (Bookings are necessary)

Travelling Supporters' Information:
Routes: The ground is situated to the North-East of Cheltenham, 1 mile from the Town Centre off the B4632 (Prestbury Road)
– Whaddon Road is to the East of the B4632 just North of Pittville Circus. Road signs in the vicinity indicate 'Whaddon Road/
Cheltenham Town FC'.

CHESTER CITY FC

Founded: 1885
Former Names: Chester FC
Nickname: 'Blues' 'City'
Ground: The Saunders Honda (Deva) Stadium, Bumpers Lane, Chester CH1 4LT
Telephone Nº: (01244) 371376
Record Attendance: 5,987 (17th April 2004)
Pitch Size: 115 × 75 yards

Colours: Blue and White striped shirts, Blue shorts
Ticket Office: (01244) 371376
Fax Number: (01244) 390265
Ground Capacity: 6,012
Seating Capacity: 3,408
Web site: www.chestercityfc.net

GENERAL INFORMATION

Car Parking: Ample available at the ground (£3.00)
Coach Parking: Available at the ground
Nearest Railway Station: Chester (2 miles)
Nearest Bus Station: Chester (1½ miles)
Club Shop: At the ground
Opening Times: Weekdays & matchdays 10.00am–5.00pm
Telephone Nº: (01244) 371376
Police Telephone Nº: (01244) 350222

GROUND INFORMATION

Away Supporters' Entrances & Sections:
South Terrace for covered accommodation and part of the West Stand for seating

ADMISSION INFO (2007/2008 PRICES)

Adult Standing: £14.00
Adult Seating: £16.00
Child/Senior Citizen Standing: £4.00 and £9.00
Child/Senior Citizen Seating: £5.00 and £11.00
Programme Price: £2.50

DISABLED INFORMATION

Wheelchairs: 72 spaces in total for Home and Away fans in the disabled areas, West Stand and East Stand
Helpers: One helper admitted per disabled person
Prices: Free for the disabled. Concessionary rates for helpers
Disabled Toilets: Available in West and East Stands
Contact: (01244) 371376   (Bookings are necessary)

Travelling Supporters' Information:
Routes: From the North: Take the M56, A41 or A56 into the Town Centre and then follow Queensferry (A548) signs into Sealand Road. Turn left at the traffic lights by 'Texas' into Bumpers Lane – the ground is ½ mile at the end of the road; From the East: Take the A54 or A51 into the Town Centre (then as North); From the South: Take the A41 or A483 into Town Centre (then as North); From the West: Take the A55, A494 or A548 and follow Queensferry signs towards Birkenhead (A494) and after 1¼ miles bear left onto the A548 (then as North); From the M6/M56 (Avoiding Town Centre): Take the M56 to Junction 16 (signposted Queensferry), turn left at the roundabout onto A5117, signposted Wales. At the next roundabout turn left onto the A5480 (signposted Chester) and after approximately 3 miles take the 3rd exit from the roundabout (signposted Sealand Road Industrial Parks). Go straight across 2 sets of traffic lights into Bumpers Lane. The ground is ½ mile on the right.

CHESTERFIELD FC

Founded: 1866 (**Entered League**: 1899)
Former Names: Chesterfield Municipal FC, Chesterfield Town FC
Nickname: 'Spireites' 'Blues'
Ground: Recreation Ground, Saltergate, Chesterfield   S40 4SX
Ground Capacity: 8,502
Seating Capacity: 3,866

Record Attendance: 30,968 (7/4/39)
Pitch Size: 112 × 73 yards
Colours: Blue shirts with White shorts
Telephone Nº: (01246) 209765
Ticket Office: (01246) 209765
Fax Number: (01246) 556799
Web Site: www.chesterfield-fc.co.uk

GENERAL INFORMATION

Car Parking: Saltergate Car Parks (½ mile)
Coach Parking: By Police direction
Nearest Railway Station: Chesterfield (1 mile)
Nearest Bus Station: Chesterfield
Club Shop: At the ground
Opening Times: Monday to Friday 9.00am to 5.00pm. Saturday 9.00am to 3.00pm on matchdays only
Telephone Nº: (01246) 209765
Police Telephone Nº: (01246) 220100

GROUND INFORMATION

Away Supporters' Entrances & Sections:
Cross Street turnstiles for Cross Street End (open) and Cross Street Inner Wing Stand (seated)

ADMISSION INFO (2007/2008 PRICES)

Adult Standing: £15.00
Adult Seating: £17.00 – £19.00
Child Standing: £5.00
Senior Citizen/Child Seating: £12.00 – £14.00 (£3.00 in the Family Stand or £7.00 in the Compton Street Stand)
Senior Citizen Standing: £9.00
Programme Price: £2.50

DISABLED INFORMATION

Wheelchairs: Approximately 15 spaces each for Home fans under the Saltergate Wing Stand and for Away fans under the Cross Street Inner Wing Stand
Helpers: One helper admitted per disabled person
Prices: Normal prices for disabled. Helpers admitted free
Disabled Toilets: One available underneath the Main Stand
Contact: (01246) 209765   (Bookings are necessary)

Travelling Supporters' Information:
Routes: From the North: Exit the M1 at Junction 30 then take the A619 into the Town Centre. Follow signs for Old Brampton into Saltergate; From the South and East: Take the A617 into the Town Centre (then as from the North); From the West: Take the A619 and when into the Town take the 1st exit at the roundabout into Foljambe Road. Follow to the end of the road, then turn right into Saltergate.

COLCHESTER UNITED FC

Founded: 1937 (**Entered League:** 1950)
Former Names: The Eagles FC & Colchester Town FC
Nickname: 'U's'
Ground: Layer Road Ground, Colchester   CO2 7JJ
Ground Capacity: 6,301
Seating Capacity: 2,115
Record Attendance: 19,072 (27/11/48)
Pitch Size: 111 × 71 yards

Colours: Royal blue & white striped shirts with Royal blue shorts and white socks
Telephone Nº: 0871 226-2161
Ticket Office: 0871 226-2161
Fax Number: (01206) 715327
Web Site: www.cu-fc.com

GENERAL INFORMATION

Car Parking: Street parking only (parking restrictions apply near the ground)
Coach Parking: Drivers should liaise with with stewards upon arrival at the ground
Nearest Railway Station: Colchester North (2 miles)
Nearest Bus Station: Colchester Town Centre
Club Shop: At the ground
Opening Times: Monday to Friday and Matchdays from 9.30am – 5.00pm
Telephone Nº: (01206) 715309
Police Telephone Nº: (01206) 762212

GROUND INFORMATION

Away Supporters' Entrances & Sections:
Layer Road End turnstiles

ADMISSION INFO (2007/2008 PRICES)

Adult Standing: £19.00
Adult Seating: £23.00
Child Standing: £5.00 to £12.00
Child Seating: £10.00 to £15.00
Concessionary Standing: £12.00
Concessionary Seating: £15.00
Programme Price: £3.00

DISABLED INFORMATION

Wheelchairs: 17 spaces for Home fans and 3 spaces for Away fans on the Terrace next to the Main Stand
Helpers: One helper admitted per wheelchair
Prices: £15.00 for the wheelchair disabled. Helpers are admitted free of charge
Disabled Toilets: Available under the Main Stand
Commentaries are available for up to 2 people
Contact: 0871 226-2161   (Bookings are required)

Travelling Supporters' Information:
Routes: From the North: Take the A134, B1508 or A12 into the Town Centre then follow signs to Layer (B1026) into Layer Road; From the South: Take the A12 and follow signs to Layer (B1026) into Layer Road; From the West: Take the A1124 or A120 into the Town Centre then follow signs to Layer (B1026) into Layer Road.

COVENTRY CITY FC

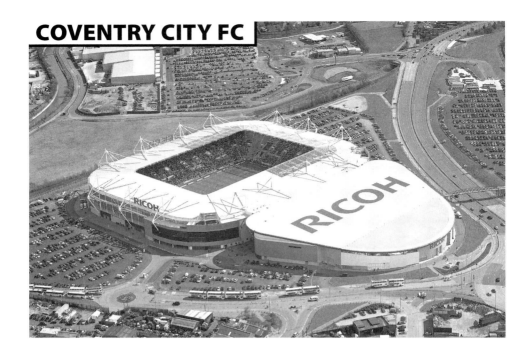

Founded: 1883 (**Entered League**: 1919)
Former Names: Singers FC (1883-1898)
Nickname: 'Sky Blues'
Ground: Ricoh Arena, Phoenix Way, Foleshill, Coventry   CV6 6GE
Ground Capacity: 32,609 (All seats)
Record Attendance: 51,455 (At Highfield Road)
Pitch Size: 110 × 75 yards

Colours: Sky blue and shadow striped shirts with Sky Blue shorts and socks
Telephone Nº: (0870) 421-1987
Ticket Office: (0870) 421-1987
Fax Numbers: (0870) 421-1988 (General Office); (0870) 421-5072 (Ticket Office)
Web Site: www.ccfc.co.uk

GENERAL INFORMATION

Car Parking: 2,000 spaces available at the ground
Coach Parking: At the ground (Car Park 'C')
Nearest Railway Station: Coventry (3 miles)
Nearest Bus Station: Coventry (3 miles)
Club Shop: At the ground
Opening Times: Weekday office hours and Matchdays
Telephone Nº: (0870) 421-1987
Police Telephone Nº: (024) 7653-9010

GROUND INFORMATION

Away Supporters' Entrances & Sections:
Turnstiles 1-11

ADMISSION INFO (2007/2008 PRICES)

Adult Seating: £20.00 – £23.00
Child Seating: £5.00 – £10.00
Programme Price: £3.00

DISABLED INFORMATION

Wheelchairs: 94 spaces available
Helpers: Admitted
Prices: £12.00 for each disabled fan with helper admitted free
Disabled Toilets: Available
Contact: (0870) 421-1987   (Bookings are necessary)

Travelling Supporters' Information:
Routes: From All Parts: Exit the M6 at Junction 3 and follow the A444 towards Coventry. The ground is located just 400 yards along this road.

CREWE ALEXANDRA FC

Founded: 1877 (**Entered League:** 1892)
Nickname: 'Railwaymen'
Ground: Alexandra Stadium, Gresty Road, Crewe, Cheshire CW2 6EB
Ground Capacity: 10,107 (All seats)
Record Attendance: 20,000 (30/1/60)
Pitch Size: 112 × 74 yards

Colours: Red shirts with White shorts
Telephone Nº: (01270) 213014
Ticket Office: (01270) 252610
Fax Number: (01270) 216320
Web Site: www.crewealex.net

GENERAL INFORMATION

Car Parking: Car Park at the ground (spaces for 400 cars)
Coach Parking: Car Park at the ground
Nearest Railway Station: Crewe (5 minutes walk)
Nearest Bus Station: Crewe Town
Club Shop: At the ground
Opening Times: Monday to Friday and Matchdays 9.00am – 5.00pm (until 7.45pm for Night matches)
Telephone Nº: (01270) 213014 extension 101
Police Telephone Nº: (01270) 500222

GROUND INFORMATION

Away Supporters' Entrances & Sections:
BMW Blue Bell Stand

ADMISSION INFO (2007/2008 PRICES)

Adult Seating: £19.00
Senior Citizen Seating: £15.00
Child Seating: £4.50 – £8.50
Programme Price: £2.50

DISABLED INFORMATION

Wheelchairs: Over 70 spaces available in total for home and away fans around the ground
Helpers: One helper admitted per disabled person
Prices: £15.00 for each disabled fan and helper
Disabled Toilets: Available in all Stands
Commentaries are available for the blind
Contact: (01270) 252610 (Bookings are necessary)

Travelling Supporters' Information:
Routes: From the North: Exit the M6 at Junction 17 and take the Crewe (A534) road, and at Crewe roundabout follow signs for Chester into Nantwich Road. Then take a left turn into Gresty Road; From the South and East: Take the A52 to the A5020, then on to Crewe roundabout (then as from the North); From the West: Take the A534 into Crewe and turn right just before the railway station into Gresty Road.

CRYSTAL PALACE FC

Founded: 1905 (Entered League: 1920)
Nickname: 'Eagles'
Ground: Selhurst Park, London   SE25 6PU
Ground Capacity: 26,247 (All seats)
Record Attendance: 51,482 (11/5/79)
Pitch Size: 110 × 74 yards

Colours: Red and Blue striped shirts with Red shorts
Telephone No: (020) 8768-6000
Ticket Office: (0871) 200-0071
Fax Number: (020) 8771-5311
Web Site: www.cpfc.co.uk

GENERAL INFORMATION

Car Parking: Street Parking and in the Sainsburys Car Park near to the ground
Coach Parking: Thornton Heath
Nearest Railway Station: Selhurst or Norwood Junction (both 5 minutes walk)
Nearest Bus Station: West Croydon
Club Shop: At the ground
Opening Times: Weekdays & Matchdays 9.00am to 6.00pm
Telephone No: (020) 8768-6100
Police Telephone No: (020) 8768-1212

GROUND INFORMATION

Away Supporters' Entrances & Sections:
Park Road for the Arthur Wait Stand

ADMISSION INFO (2007/2008 PRICES)

Adult Seating: £25.00 – £30.00
Child Seating: £10.00 – £15.00
Programme Price: £3.00

DISABLED INFORMATION

Wheelchairs: Spaces are available in the disabled area, Holmesdale Road Stand and also in the Arthur Wait Stand
Helpers: One helper admitted per wheelchair
Prices: Normal prices apply for the disabled. Helpers are admitted free of charge
Disabled Toilets: Located in the disabled section
Commentaries are available for 12 people
Contact: (020) 8768-6081   (Bookings are necessary)

Travelling Supporters' Information:
Routes: From the North: Take the M1/A1 to the North Circular (A406) for Chiswick. Take the South Circular (A205) to Wandsworth then the A3 to the A214 and follow signs for Streatham to the A23. Turn left onto the B273 after 1 mile, follow to the end, turn left into the High Street and then into Whitehorse Lane; From the East: Take the A232 (Croydon Road) to Shirley and join the A215 (Northwood Road). After 2¼ miles turn left into Whitehorse Lane; From the South: Take the A23 and follow signs for Crystal Palace (B266) through Thornton Heath into Whitehorse Lane; From the West: Take the M4 to Chiswick (then as North).

DAGENHAM & REDBRIDGE FC

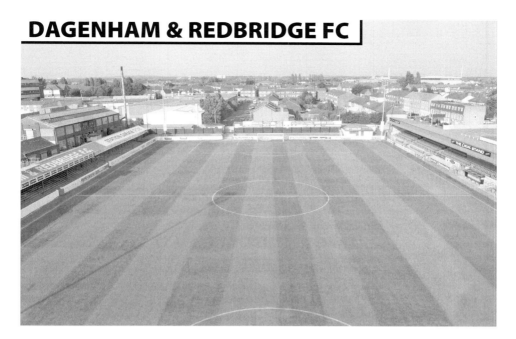

Founded: 1992   (Entered League: 2007)
Former Names: Formed by the merger of
Dagenham FC and Redbridge Forest FC
Nickname: 'The Daggers'
Ground: Glyn Hopkin Stadium, Victoria Road,
Dagenham, Essex RM10 7XL
Record Attendance: 7,100 (1967)
Pitch Size: 110 × 65 yards

Colours: Red shirts with White shorts
Telephone Nº: (0208) 592-1549
Office Phone Nº: (0208) 592-7194
Secretary's Phone Nº: (0208) 592-7194
Fax Number: (0208) 593-7227
Ground Capacity: 6,077
Seating Capacity: 1,015
Web site: www.daggers.co.uk

GENERAL INFORMATION

Supporters Club: Russell Elmes, 24 Brewood, Dagenham,
RM8 2BL
Telephone Nº: (0208) 593-2801
Car Parking: Street parking only
Coach Parking: Street parking only
Nearest Railway Station: Dagenham East (5 mins. walk)
Nearest Bus Station: Romford
Club Shop: At the ground
Opening Times: Matchdays only
Telephone Nº: (0208) 592-7194
Police Telephone Nº: (0208) 593-8232

GROUND INFORMATION

Away Supporters' Entrances & Sections:
Pondfield Road entrances for Pondfield Road End

ADMISSION INFO (2007/2008 PRICES)

Adult Standing: £15.00
Adult Seating: £18.00 – £19.00
Under-16s Standing: £10.00
Child Seating: £10.00 – £13.00 (£7.00 in the Family Stand)
Senior Citizen Seating: £7.00 in the Family Stand
Note: Discounts are available for advance purchases
Programme Price: £2.50

DISABLED INFORMATION

Wheelchairs: Accommodated in front of new Stand
Helpers: Admitted
Prices: £10.00 for the disabled. Free of charge for Helpers
Disabled Toilets: Available at the East and West ends of the
ground and also in the Clubhouse
Contact: (0208) 592-7194   (Bookings are necessary)

Travelling Supporters' Information:
Routes: From the North & West: Take the M11 to its end and join the A406 South. At the large roundabout take the slip road
on the left signposted A13 to Dagenham. As you approach Dagenham, stay in the left lane and follow signs for A1306 signposted
Dagenham East. Turn left onto the A1112 at the 3rd set of traffic lights by the McDonalds. Proceed along Ballards Road to The
Bull roundabout and bear left. Victoria Road is 450 yards on the left after passing Dagenham East tube station; From the South
& East: Follow signs for the A13 to Dagenham. Take the next slip road off signposted Elm Park & Dagenham East then turn right
at the roundabout. Go straight on at the next roundabout and turn left onto A1306. After ½ mile you will see a McDonalds on
the right. Get into the right hand filter lane and turn right onto A1112. Then as from the North & West.

DARLINGTON FC

Founded: 1883 (**Entered League**: 1921)
Nickname: 'Quakers'
Ground: 96.6 TFM Darlington Arena, Hurworth Moor,
Neasham Road, Darlington   DL2 1DL
Ground Capacity: 25,321 (All seats)
Record Attendance: 10,224 (16th August 2003)
Pitch Size: 115 × 74 yards

Colours: White and Black shirts with Black shorts
Telephone Nº: (01325) 387000
Ticket Office: (01325) 387030
Fax Number: (01325) 387050
Web Site: www.darlington-fc.net

GENERAL INFORMATION

Car Parking: Limited number of spaces at the ground
Coach Parking: At the ground
Nearest Railway Station: Darlington (1½ miles)
Nearest Bus Station: Darlington Central
Club Shop: At the ground
Opening Times: Monday to Friday 10.00am – 5.00pm and
Saturday matchdays 10.00am – 3.00pm
Telephone Nº: (01325) 387020
Police Telephone Nº: (01325) 467681

GROUND INFORMATION

Away Supporters' Entrances & Sections:
East Stand

ADMISSION INFO (2007/2008 PRICES)

Adult Seating: £16.00
Senior Citizen/Student Seating: £11.00
Child Seating: £5.00 – £7.00 (Depends on age of child)
Note: Price reductions are available if tickets are pre-booked
Programme Price: £2.50

DISABLED INFORMATION

Wheelchairs: Spaces available in disabled sections
throughout the ground. Lifts are available in the stands
Helpers: One helper admitted per disabled person
Prices: £11.00 for the disabled and blind (£10.00 if
purchased in advance). Free of charge for helpers
Disabled Toilets: Available in all stands
Contact: (01325) 387000 – Harry Sams

Travelling Supporters' Information:
Routes: From All Parts: Take the A1 to the A66(M) and follow the road to it's end. Take the 1st exit at the roundabout, go up the
hill then, at the second roundabout, take the 3rd exit signposted A66 Teeside. The ground is at the next roundabout after
approximately 1 mile.

DERBY COUNTY FC

Founded: 1884 (**Entered League:** 1888)
Nickname: 'Rams'
Ground: Pride Park Stadium, Royal Way, Pride Park, Derby   DE24 8XL
Ground Capacity: 33,597 (All seats)
Record Attendance: 33,597 (25/5/2001)
Pitch Size: 110 × 74 yards

Colours: White shirts with Black shorts
Telephone Nº: (0870) 444-1884
Ticket Office: (0870) 444-1884
Fax Number: (01332) 667519
Web Site: www.dcfc.co.uk

GENERAL INFORMATION

Car Parking: Spaces for 1,200 cars at the ground (permit holders only)
Coach Parking: At the ground
Nearest Railway Station: Derby Midland (1 mile)
Nearest Bus Station: Derby Central
Club Shop: shop dcfc at the ground
Opening Times: Weekdays and Matchdays 9.00am–6.00pm Saturdays 9.00am – 5.30pm; Sundays 10.00am – 4.00pm
Telephone Nº: (0870) 444-1884
Police Telephone Nº: (01332) 290100

GROUND INFORMATION

Away Supporters' Entrances & Sections:
South Stand (Cawarden Stand)

ADMISSION INFO (2007/2008 PRICES)

Adult Seating: £25.00 – £35.00
Child/Concessionary Seating: £9.00 – £18.00
Note: Prices vary depending on the category of the game
Programme Price: £3.00

DISABLED INFORMATION

Wheelchairs: 204 spaces available in total
Helpers: One helper admitted for each disabled fan
Prices: £25.00 – £35.00 for each disabled fan & helper
Disabled Toilets: Yes
Contact: (0870) 444-1884   (Bookings are necessary)

Travelling Supporters' Information:
Routes: From All Parts: Exit the M1 at Junction 25 and follow the A52 towards the City Centre until the ground is signposted on the left. Follow the signs for the ground.
From the Train Station: The Stadium is 10 minutes walk by way of a tunnel under the railway opposite Brunswick Inn, Station Approach. Then follow the footpath; Buses: A shuttle service runs from the bus station from 1.00pm until 2.45pm on Saturdays. A similar service runs from 6.00pm – 7.30pm for midweek games. Return shuttles are available post-match.

DONCASTER ROVERS FC

Founded: 1879
Former Names: None
Nickname: 'Rovers'
Ground: Keepmoat Stadium, Stadium Way, Doncaster   DN4 5JW
Record Attendance: 14,129 (6th January 2007)
Pitch Size: 110 × 72 yards

Colours: Red & White hooped shirts with Red shorts
Telephone Nº: (01302) 764664
Ticket Office: (01302) 762576
Fax Number: (01302) 322812
Ground Capacity: 15,000
Web site: www.doncasterroversfc.co.uk

GENERAL INFORMATION

Car Parking: 1,000 spaces available at the ground
Coach Parking: At the ground
Nearest Railway Station: Doncaster (2 miles)
Nearest Bus Station: Doncaster (2 miles)
Club Shop: At the ground
Opening Times: 10.00am to 4.00pm on weekdays
Telephone Nº: (01302) 764667
Police Telephone Nº: (01302) 366744

GROUND INFORMATION

Away Supporters' Entrances & Sections:
North Stand

ADMISSION INFO (2007/2008 PRICES)

Adult Seating: £15.00 – £22.00
Child/Senior Citizen Seating: £5.00 – £16.00
Programme Price: £2.50
Note: Prices vary depending on the category of the game

DISABLED INFORMATION

Wheelchairs: Accommodated in the West Stand
Helpers: Admitted
Prices: Concessionary prices are charged for the disabled. Helpers are admitted free of charge
Disabled Toilets: Available in the East and West Stands
Contact: (01302) 764664   (Bookings are necessary)

Travelling Supporters' Information:
Routes: Exit the M18 at Junction 3 and follow the A6182 towards Doncaster. The stadium is approximately 1½ miles from the motorway and is well signposted so follow these signs. There are 1,000 car parking spaces available at the stadium and the cost is £5.00 per car. A number of businesses on the nearby business park also offer matchday parking for a similar charge. When crowds over 9,000 are expected, a Park and Ride service runs from Doncaster Racecourse. The shuttle service buses run from 1.00pm to 3.00pm to the Stadium and from 4.30pm to 6.30pm returning to the Racecourse from the Stadium.

EVERTON FC

Founded: 1878 (**Entered League:** 1888)
Former Names: St. Domingo's FC (1878-79)
Nickname: 'The Toffees'
Ground: Goodison Park, Goodison Road, Liverpool L4 4EL
Ground Capacity: 40,565 (All seats)
Record Attendance: 78,299 (18/9/48)

Pitch Size: 110 × 74 yards
Colours: Blue shirts with White shorts
Telephone Nº: 0870 442-1878
Ticket Office: (0870) 442-1878
Fax Number: (0151) 286-9112
Web Site: www.evertonfc.com

GENERAL INFORMATION

Car Parking: Corner of Priory Road and Utting Avenue
Coach Parking: Priory Road
Nearest Railway Station: Kirkdale
Nearest Mainline Railway Station: Liverpool Lime Street
Nearest Bus Station: Queen's Square, Liverpool
Club Shop: 'Megastore' in Walton Lane by the ground
Opening Times: Weekdays 9.30am to 5.00pm, Wednesdays 10.00am to 5.00pm. Saturdays 9.00am to 5.00pm. Open one hour after matches
Telephone Nº: 0870 442-1878
Police Telephone Nº: (0151) 709-6010

GROUND INFORMATION

Away Supporters' Entrances & Sections:
Bullens Road entrances for Bullens Stand

ADMISSION INFO (2007/2008 PRICES)

Adult Seating: £28.00 – £34.00
Child Seating: £15.00 – £19.00
Senior Citizen Seating: £21.00 – £23.00
Note: Concessionary prices are only available in some areas
Programme Price: £3.00

DISABLED INFORMATION

Wheelchairs: 85 spaces for home fans, 13 spaces for away fans in the disabled section.
Helpers: One helper admitted per wheelchair
Prices: £25.00 for each disabled fan + 1 helper
Disabled Toilets: Available in the disabled section
Commentaries are available for the blind
Contact: (0870) 442-1878 (Bookings are necessary)

Travelling Supporters' Information:
Routes: From the North: Exit the M6 at Junction 26 onto the M58 and continue to it's end. Take the 2nd exit at the roundabout onto the A59 Ormskirk Road. Continue along into Rice Lane and go straight across at the next roundabout into County Road. After ½ mile, turn left into Everton Valley then bear left into Walton Lane for the ground; From the South & East: Exit the M6 at Junction 21A and take the M62 to it's end. Turn right at traffic lights onto A5088 Queen Drive and continue to the junction with Walton Hall Avenue then turn left into Walton Lane (A580) and the ground is on the right.
Bus Services: Services to the ground – 19, 20, F1, F2, 30

FULHAM FC

Founded: 1879 (**Entered League**: 1907)
Former Names: Fulham St. Andrew's FC (1879-1898)
Nickname: 'Cottagers'
Ground: Craven Cottage, Stevenage Road, Fulham, London   SW6 6HH
Ground Capacity: 24,500 (All seats)
Record Attendance: 49,335 (8/10/38)

Pitch Size: 109 × 74 yards
Colours: White shirts with Black shorts
Telephone Nº: 0870 442-1222
Ticket Office: 0870 442-1234
Fax Number: 0870 442-0236
Web Site: www.fulhamfc.com

GENERAL INFORMATION
Car Parking: Street Parking
Coach Parking: Stevenage Road
Nearest Railway Station: Putney (1 mile)
Nearest Tube Station: Putney Bridge (District) (1 mile)
Club Shop: At the ground and Fulham Road
Opening Times: At the ground: Weekends 12.00pm to 4.00pm, Matchdays with 3.00pm kick-off open 11.00am to 5.00pm; Evening Matches open 5.00pm to 10.00pm; Fulham Road: Monday to Saturday 9.00am to 5.00pm
Telephone Nº: (0870) 442-1222
Police Telephone Nº: (020) 7385-1212

GROUND INFORMATION
Away Supporters' Entrances & Sections:
Putney End for the Putney Stand

ADMISSION INFO (2007/2008 PRICES)
Adult Seating: £25.00 – £50.00
Child Seating: £5.00 – £20.00
Concessionary Seating: £15.00 – £30.00
Note: Prices vary depending on the category of the game
Programme Price: £3.00

DISABLED INFORMATION
Wheelchairs: 31 spaces for Home fans and 7 spaces for Away fans in the Putney End, Block 7
Helpers: One helper admitted per disabled person
Prices: Half-price for the disabled. Free of charge for helpers
Disabled Toilets: Available next to each disabled area
Contact: (0870) 442-1234 Option 3   (Bookings necessary)

Travelling Supporters' Information:
Routes: From the North: Take the A1/M1 to the North Circular (A406), travel west to Neasden and follow signs for Harlesdon A404, then Hammersmith A219. At Broadway, follow the Fulham sign and turn right after 1 mile into Harboard Street then left at the end for the ground; From the South & East: Take the South Circular (A205), follow the Putney Bridge sign (A219). Cross the bridge and follow Hammersmith signs for ½ mile, turn left into Bishops Park Road, then right at the end; From the West: Take the M4 to the A4. Branch left after 2 miles into Hammersmith Broadway (then as from the North).

GILLINGHAM FC

Founded: 1893 (**Entered League:** 1920)
Former Names: New Brompton FC (1893-1913)
Nickname: 'Gills'
Ground: Priestfield Stadium, Redfern Avenue, Gillingham, Kent   ME7 4DD
Ground Capacity: 11,500 (All seats)
Record Attendance: 23,002 (10/1/48)

Pitch Size: 114 × 75 yards
Telephone Nº: (01634) 300000
Ticket Office: (01634) 300000
Fax Number: (01634) 850986
Web Site: www.gillinghamfootballclub.co.uk

GENERAL INFORMATION
Car Parking: Street parking
Coach Parking: By Police direction
Nearest Railway Station: Gillingham
Nearest Bus Station: Gillingham
Club Shop: Megastore in Redfern Avenue
Opening Times: Megastore is open Weekdays and Matchdays from 9.00am to 5.00pm
Telephone Nº: (01634) 300000
Police Telephone Nº: (01634) 891005

GROUND INFORMATION
Away Supporters' Entrances & Sections:
Priestfield Road End

ADMISSION INFO (2007/2008 PRICES)
Adult Seating: £20.00 – £25.00
Senior Citizen/Student Seating: £14.00 – £25.00
Child Seating (Ages 11-16): £12.00
Child Seating (Ages 7-11): £5.00 – £7.00
Note: Discounts are available for tickets purchased in advance
Programme Price: £2.50

DISABLED INFORMATION
Wheelchairs: 65 spaces in total for Home and Away fans and helpers in disabled sections around the ground
Helpers: One helper admitted per disabled person
Prices: Normal prices for the disabled. Free for helpers
Disabled Toilets: Available in the Gordon Road Stand
Contact: (01634) 300000 (Bookings are necessary)

Travelling Supporters' Information:
Routes: From All Parts: Exit the M2 at Junction 4 and follow the link road (dual carriageway) B278 to the 3rd roundabout. Turn left onto the A2 (dual carriageway) and go across the roundabout to the traffic lights. Turn right into Woodlands Road after the traffic lights. The ground is ¼ mile on the left.

GRIMSBY TOWN FC |

Founded: 1878 **(Entered League:** 1892)
Former Names: Grimsby Pelham FC (1879)
Nickname: 'Mariners'
Ground: Blundell Park, Cleethorpes   DN35 7PY
Ground Capacity: 8,974 (All seats)
Record Attendance: 31,651 (20/2/37)
Pitch Size: 111 × 74 yards

Colours: Black and White striped shirts, Black shorts
Telephone Nº: (01472) 605050
Ticket Office: (01472) 605050
Fax Number: (01472) 693665
Web Site: www.gtfc.co.uk

GENERAL INFORMATION

Car Parking: Street parking
Coach Parking: Harrington Street – near the ground
Nearest Railway Station: Cleethorpes (1½ miles)
Nearest Bus Station: Brighowgate, Grimsby (4 miles)
Club Shop: At the ground
Opening Times: Monday – Friday 9.00am to 5.00pm;
Matchday Saturdays 9.00am to kick-off
Telephone Nº: (01472) 605050
Police Telephone Nº: (01472) 359171

GROUND INFORMATION

Away Supporters' Entrances & Sections:
Harrington Street turnstiles 15-18 and Constitution Avenue
turnstiles 5-14

ADMISSION INFO (2007/2008 PRICES)

Adult Seating: £16.00 – £18.00 (Away fans £18.00)
Senior Citizens/Young Adults: £12.00
Child Seating: £8.00 (Under-15s)
Programme Price: £2.50

DISABLED INFORMATION

Wheelchairs: 50 spaces in total for Home and Away fans in
the disabled section, in front of the Main Stand
Helpers: Helpers are admitted
Prices: £11.00 each for the disabled and helpers
Disabled Toilets: Available in disabled section
Commentaries are available in disabled section
Contact: (01472) 605050   (Bookings are necessary)

Travelling Supporters' Information:
Routes: From All Parts except Lincolnshire and East Anglia: Take the M180 to the A180 and follow signs for Grimsby/
Cleethorpes. The A180 ends at a roundabout (the 3rd in short distance after crossing docks), take the 2nd exit from the roundabout
over the Railway flyover into Cleethorpes Road (A1098) and continue into Grimsby Road. After the second stretch of dual
carriageway, the ground is ½ mile on the left; From Lincolnshire: Take the A46 or A16 and follow Cleethorpes signs along
(A1098) Weelsby Road for 2 miles. Take the 1st exit at the roundabout at the end of Clee Road into Grimsby Road. The ground is
1¾ miles on the right.

HARTLEPOOL UNITED FC

Founded: 1908 (**Entered League:** 1921)
Former Names: Hartlepools United FC (1908-68); Hartlepool FC (1968-77)
Nickname: 'The Pool' 'Pools'
Ground: Victoria Park, Clarence Road, Hartlepool, TS24 8BZ
Ground Capacity: 7,629
Seating Capacity: 4,175

Record Attendance: 17,426 (15/1/57)
Pitch Size: 110 × 80 yards
Colours: Blue and White striped shirts, Blue shorts
Telephone Nº: (01429) 272584
Ticket Office: (01429) 272584 Extension 2
Ticket Office e-mail: tickets@hartlepoolunited.co.uk
Fax Number: (01429) 863007
Web Site: www.hartlepoolunited.co.uk

GENERAL INFORMATION

Car Parking: Limited space at the ground (£6.00 charge) and also street parking
Coach Parking: Church Street
Nearest Railway Station: Hartlepool Church Street (5 minutes walk)
Club Shop: At the ground
Opening Times: Weekdays 9.00am to 5.00pm; non-match Saturdays 9.00am to 1.00pm. Saturday matchdays 10.00am–3.00pm and 4.30pm–5.30pm
Telephone Nº: (01429) 260491
Police Telephone Nº: (01429) 221151

GROUND INFORMATION

Away Supporters' Entrances & Sections:
Clarence Road turnstiles 1 & 2 for Rink End

ADMISSION INFO (2007/2008 PRICES)

Adult Standing: £18.00
Adult Seating: £20.00
Child/Senior Citizen Standing: £9.00
Child/Senior Citizen Seating: £10.00 (£8.00 Family Stand)
Programme Price: £2.50

DISABLED INFORMATION

Wheelchairs: 21 spaces for Home fans in disabled section, Cyril Knowles Stand, 10 spaces for Away fans in the Rink End
Helpers: One helper admitted per wheelchair
Prices: £20.00 for the Disabled. Helpers free of charge
Disabled Toilets: Available in the Cyril Knowles Stand
Contact: (01429) 272584 (Bookings are advisable)

Travelling Supporters' Information: Routes: From the North: Take the A1/A19 to the A179 and follow Town Centre/Marina signs. Turn right at the roundabout by the 'Historic Quayside' and cross over the Railway bridge. The ground is on the left; From the South & West: Take the A689 following Town Centre/Marina signs. Turn left at the roundabout by the 'Historic Quayside' and cross over the Railway bridge. The ground is on the left.

HEREFORD UNITED FC

Founded: 1924
Former Names: None
Nickname: 'United' 'The Bulls'
Ground: Edgar Street, Hereford   HR4 9JU
Record Attendance: 18,114 (4/1/58)
Pitch Size: 112 × 78 yards

Colours: White shirts with White shorts
Telephone No: (01432) 276666
Fax Number: (01432) 341359
Ground Capacity: 7,873
Seating Capacity: 2,761
Web site: www.herefordunited.co.uk

GENERAL INFORMATION

Supporters Club: None
Car Parking: Merton Meadow Car Park
Coach Parking: Cattle Market (Near the ground)
Nearest Railway Station: Hereford (½ mile)
Nearest Bus Station: Commercial Road, Hereford
Club Shop: At the ground
Opening Times: Weekdays 9.00am to 4.00pm and
Matchdays 12.00pm to 3.00pm
Telephone No: (01432) 276666
Police Telephone No: (01432) 276422

GROUND INFORMATION

Away Supporters' Entrances & Sections:
Blackfriars Street and Edgar Street for the Blackfriars Street
End

ADMISSION INFO (2007/2008 PRICES)

Adult Standing: £13.00
Adult Seating: £15.00
Child Standing: £6.00
Child Seating: £7.00
Senior Citizen Standing: £9.00
Senior Citizen Seating: £12.00
Programme Price: £2.50

DISABLED INFORMATION

Wheelchairs: 10 spaces in total for Home and Away fans in
the disabled section, Merton Meadow Stand
Helpers: One helper admitted per disabled person
Prices: £12.00 for the disabled. Free of charge for helpers
Disabled Toilets: Yes
Contact: (01432) 276666   (Bookings are not necessary)

Travelling Supporters' Information:
Routes: From the North: Follow A49 Hereford signs straight into Edgar Street; From the East: Take the A465 or A438 into
Hereford Town Centre, then follow signs for Leominster (A49) into Edgar Street; From the South: Take the A49 or A45 into the
Town Centre (then as East); From the West: Take the A438 into the Town Centre (then as East).

HUDDERSFIELD TOWN FC

Founded: 1908 **(Entered League:** 1910)
Nickname: 'Terriers'
Ground: The Galpharm Stadium, Huddersfield, HD1 6PX
Ground Capacity: 24,554 (All seats)
Record Attendance: 23,678 (12/12/99)
Pitch Size: 115 × 76 yards

Colours: Blue and White striped shirts, White shorts
Telephone Nº: 0870 444-4677
Ticket Office: 0870 444-4552
Fax Number: (01484) 484101
Web Site: www.htafc.com

GENERAL INFORMATION

Car Parking: Car park for 1,100 cars adjacent (pre-sold)
Coach Parking: Adjacent car park
Nearest Railway Station: Huddersfield (1¼ miles)
Nearest Bus Station: Huddersfield
Club Shop: At the ground and in the Town Centre
Opening Times: Weekdays 9.00am to 5.00pm and Saturday Matchdays 9.00am to 3.00pm
Telephone Nº: (01484) 484144 or 421612
Police Telephone Nº: (01484) 422122

GROUND INFORMATION

Away Supporters' Entrances & Sections:
Pink Link Stand

ADMISSION INFO (2007/2008 PRICES)

Adult Seating: £19.00 – £22.00
Child Seating: £7.00 – £10.00
Senior Citizen/Student Seating: £10.00 – £13.00
Note: Tickets are cheaper if bought prior to the matchday
Programme Price: £3.00

DISABLED INFORMATION

Wheelchairs: 254 spaces in total for home and away fans in the disabled sections, Lawrence Batley Lower Stand, Pink Link Stand and Antich Stand. Additional spaces are available for the ambulant disabled and visually impaired.
Helpers: Admitted
Prices: £11.00 for the disabled. Free of charge for helpers
Disabled Toilets: Available in the disabled sections
Commentaries are available for the blind.
Contact: 0870 444-4552 (Bookings are necessary)

Travelling Supporters' Information:
Routes: From the North, East and West: Exit the M62 at Junction 25 and take the A644 and A62 following Huddersfield signs. Follow signs for the Galpharm Stadium; From the South: Leave the M1 at Junction 38 and follow the A637/A642 to Huddersfield. At the Ring Road, follow signs for the A62 to the Galpharm Stadium.

HULL CITY AFC

Founded: 1904 (**Entered League**: 1905)
Nickname: 'Tigers'
Ground: The Kingston Communications Stadium, The Circle, Walton Street, Hull   HU3 6HU
Ground Capacity: 25,404 (All seats)
Record Attendance: 24,004 (2nd June 2003)
Pitch Size: 115 × 75 yards

Colours: Black and Amber shirts with Black shorts
Telephone Nº: (0870) 837-0003
Ticket Office: (0870) 837-0004
Fax Number: (01482) 304882
Web Site: www.hullcityafc.net

GENERAL INFORMATION

Car Parking: Walton Street Car Park (£2.50), City Centre Car Parks and a Park & Ride scheme from Priory Park (£1.20)
Coach Parking: By Police direction
Nearest Railway Station: Hull Paragon
Nearest Bus Station: City Centre, Hull
Club Shop: Tiger Leisure Superstore at the Stadium
Opening Times: Monday to Saturday 9.00am to 5.00pm. Open until 5.30pm on Saturday matchdays
Telephone Nº: (0870) 837-0005
Police Telephone Nº: (01482) 220148

GROUND INFORMATION

Away Supporters' Entrances & Sections: North Stand

ADMISSION INFO (2007/2008 PRICES)

Adult Seating: £17.00 – £23.00
Child Seating: £9.00 – £14.00
Concessionary Seating: £12.00 – £14.00
Programme Price: £2.50

DISABLED INFORMATION

Wheelchairs: 304 spaces in total for Home and Away fans available around all the stands at both upper and lower level
Helpers: One helper admitted per disabled person
Prices: Concessionary rates for the disabled. Free for helpers
Disabled Toilets: Many available throughout the ground. Lifts are available. Commentaries are available for the blind
Contact: (0870) 837-0003   (Bookings are not necessary)

Travelling Supporters' Information:
Routes: From the West: Take the M62 then join the A63. Continue under the Humber Bridge as the road becomes the A63 Clive Sullivan Way and turn off at the slip road just before the flyover marked "Local Traffic/Infirmary". Take the 2nd exit at the roundabout into Rawling Way. Turn left at the next main set of traffic lights on A1105 Anlaby Road. Continue over the flyover then take a right turn into Walton Street. The car park is half way down this street after the Sports Arena; From the Humber Bridge: Follow signs for Hull City Centre – the road curves round to the left to join the A63 Clive Sullivan Way. Then as from the West; From the North: Take the A1079 towards Beverley then follow signs for the Humber Bridge and A164. Take the A63 sign-posted Hull City Centre and follow onto the A63 Clive Sullivan Way. Then as from the West.

IPSWICH TOWN FC

Founded: 1878 (**Entered League:** 1938)
Nickname: 'Town' 'Tractor Boys'
Ground: Portman Road, Ipswich IP1 2DA
Ground Capacity: 30,311 (All seats)
Record Attendance: 38,010 (8/3/75)
Pitch Size: 112 × 72 yards

Colours: Blue shirts with White shorts
Telephone Nº: (01473) 400500
Ticket Office: (0870) 1110555
Fax Number: (01473) 400040
Web Site: www.itfc.co.uk

GENERAL INFORMATION

Car Parking: Portman Road & Sir Alf Ramsey Way car parks
Coach Parking: Bibb Way
Nearest Railway Station: Ipswich (5 minutes walk)
Nearest Bus Station: Ipswich
Club Shop: At the ground
Opening Times: Weekdays and Matchdays 9.00am–5.00pm
Telephone Nº: (01473) 400501
Police Telephone Nº: (01473) 233000

GROUND INFORMATION

Away Supporters' Entrances & Sections:
Cobbold Stand

ADMISSION INFO (2007/2008 PRICES)

Adult Seating: £25.00 – £48.50
Child Seating: £7.50 – £24.00
Senior Citizen Seating: £18.00 – £37.00
Note: Discounts are available for advance ticket purchases.
Programme Price: £3.00

DISABLED INFORMATION

Wheelchairs: 120 spaces and 130 seats for home fans, 10 spaces and 10 seats for away fans in the Britannia, Greene King and North Stands upper and lower tiers
Helpers: One helper admitted per disabled person
Prices: Adult price charged for disabled fan + one helper.
Disabled Toilets: Adjacent to the disabled areas
Commentaries are available for the blind
Contact: (0870) 1110555   (Bookings are necessary)

Travelling Supporters' Information:
Routes: From the North and West: Take the A1214 from the A14/A12 following signs for Ipswich West only. Proceed through Holiday Inn Hotel traffic lights and at the 3rd set of traffic lights turn right into West End Road. The ground is ¼ mile along on the left; From the South: Follow signs for Ipswich West, then as from the North and West above.

LEEDS UNITED FC

Founded: 1919 (**Entered League**: 1920)
Former Names: Formed after Leeds City FC were wound up for 'Irregular Practices'
Nickname: 'United'
Ground: Elland Road, Leeds   LS11 0ES
Ground Capacity: 39,460 (All seats)
Record Attendance: 57,892 (15/3/67)

Pitch Size: 115 × 74 yards
Colours: White shirts and shorts
Telephone Nº: (0113) 367-6000
Ticket Office: (0845) 1211992
Fax Number: (0113) 367-6050
Web Site: www.leedsunited.com

GENERAL INFORMATION

Car Parking: Large car parks adjacent to the Stadium
Coach Parking: Adjacent to the Stadium
Nearest Railway Station: Leeds City (1½ miles)
Nearest Bus Station: Leeds City Centre – specials from Swinegate
Club Shop: At the South East corner of the Stadium
Opening Times: Weekdays 9.00am to 5.00pm, Matchdays 9.00am to one hour after the final whistle
Telephone Nº: (0113) 367-6221
Police Telephone Nº: (0845) 6060606

GROUND INFORMATION

Away Supporters' Entrances & Sections:
South East Corner or South Stand – Upper & Lower Tiers

ADMISSION INFO (2007/2008 PRICES)

Adult Seating: £15.00 – £30.00
Child Seating: £10.00 (In the Family Stand only)
Senior Citizen Seating: £11.00 – £16.00
Note: Prices vary according to the category of game played.
Programme Price: £3.00

DISABLED INFORMATION

Wheelchairs: 131 spaces in total in the disabled sections, West, North and South Stands
Helpers: One helper admitted per disabled person
Prices: Please contact the club for details
Disabled Toilets: Adjacent to each of the disabled sections
Commentaries via headphones in the West Stand
Contact: (0113) 367-6178 (Ms. Tracey Lazenby)
(Bookings are necessary)

Travelling Supporters' Information:
Routes: From the North: Take the A58 or A61 into the City Centre and follow signs to the M621. Leave the Motorway after 1½ miles and exit the roundabout onto the A643 into Elland Road; From the North-East: Take the A63 or A64 into the City Centre (then as from the North); From the South: Take the M1 to the M621 (then as from the North); From the West: Take the M62 to the M621 (then as from the North).

LEICESTER CITY FC

Founded: 1884 (**Entered League:** 1894)
Former Names: Leicester Fosse FC (1884-1919)
Nickname: 'Foxes'
Ground: Walkers Stadium, Filbert Way, Leicester, LE2 7FL
Ground Capacity: 32,500 (All seats)
Record Attendance: 32,148

Pitch Size: 110 × 72 yards
Colours: Blue shirts and shorts
Telephone N°: (0870) 040-6000
Ticket Office: (0870) 499-1884
Fax Number: (0116) 229-4404
Web Site: www.lcfc.com

GENERAL INFORMATION
Car Parking: NCP Car Park (5 minutes walk)
Coach Parking: Sawday Street
Nearest Railway Station: Leicester (1 mile)
Nearest Bus Station: St. Margaret's (1 mile)
Club Shop: At the ground
Opening Times: Weekdays and Matchdays 9.00am–5.30pm
Telephone N°: (0870) 040-6000
Police Telephone N°: (0116) 222-2222

GROUND INFORMATION
Away Supporters' Entrances & Sections:
At the corner of the North and East Stands

ADMISSION INFO (2007/2008 PRICES)
Adult Seating: £23.00 – £30.00
Child Seating: £10.00
Senior Citizen Seating: £21.00
Programme Price: £3.00

DISABLED INFORMATION
Wheelchairs: 186 spaces for the disabled + 111 spaces for helpers accommodated at various levels in all stands
Helpers: One carer admitted per disabled person
Prices: Reduced prices are available – Phone for details
Disabled Toilets: Available in all stands
Contact: (0870) 040-6000 (Hayley Mason – phone or fax)

Travelling Supporters' Information:
Routes: From the North: Take the A46/A607 into the City Centre or exit the M1 at Junction 21, take the A5460, turn right ¾ mile after the Railway Bridge into Upperton Road, then right into Filbert Way; From the East: Take the A47 into the City Centre (then as from the North); From the South: Exit the M1 at Junction 21 and take the A5460, turn right ¾ mile after Railway Bridge into Upperton Road, then right into Filbert Way; From the West: Take the M69 to the City Centre (then as from North).

LEYTON ORIENT FC

Founded: 1881 (**Entered League:** 1905)
Former Names: Glyn Cricket and Football Club (1881-86); Eagle FC (1886-88); Clapton Orient FC (1888-1946); Leyton Orient FC (1946-66); Orient FC (1966-87)
Nickname: 'O's'
Ground: Matchroom Stadium, Brisbane Road, Leyton, London   E10 5NF

Ground Capacity: Approximately 9,300 (all seats)
Record Attendance: 34,345 (21/1/64)
Pitch Size: 110 × 76 yards
Telephone Nº: 0871 310-1881
Ticket Office: 0871 310-1883
Fax Number: 0871 310-1882
Web Site: www.leytonorient.com

GENERAL INFORMATION
Car Parking: Street parking
Coach Parking: By Police direction
Nearest Railway Station: Leyton Midland Road (½ mile)
Nearest Tube Station: Leyton (Central)
Club Shop: At the ground
Opening Times: Weekdays 9.30am to 4.30pm
Telephone Nº: 0871 310-1889
Police Telephone Nº: (020) 8556-8855

GROUND INFORMATION
Away Supporters' Entrances & Sections:
East Stand

ADMISSION INFO (2007/2008 PRICES)
Adult Seating: £20.00 to £22.00
Child Seating: £5.00 to £14.00 (Free for the Under-11s in the North Family Stand)
Senior Citizen Seating: £13.00 to £14.00
Programme Price: £3.00

DISABLED INFORMATION
Wheelchairs: Spaces are available in the North, East and West Stands
Helpers: One helper admitted per disabled person
Prices: Free of charge for the disabled
Disabled Toilets: Available near disabled sections
Contact: 0871 310-1883   (Bookings are necessary)

Travelling Supporters' Information:
Routes: From the North & West: Take A406 North Circular, follow signs for Chelmsford to Edmonton. After 2½ miles take the 3rd exit at the roundabout towards Leyton (A112). Pass the railway station, turn right after ½ mile into Windsor Road and left into Brisbane Road; From the East: Follow the A12 to London then the City for Leytonstone. Follow Hackney signs into Grove Road, cross Main Road into Ruckholt Road then turn right into Leyton High Road, turn left after ¼ mile into Buckingham Road and left into Brisbane Road; From the South: Take the A102M through the Blackwall Tunnel, follow signs for Newmarket (A102) to join the A11 to Stratford, then follow signs for Stratford Station into Leyton Road to the railway station (then as from North).

LINCOLN CITY FC

Founded: 1884 (**Entered League:** 1892)
Nickname: 'Red Imps'
Ground: Sincil Bank Stadium, Lincoln LN5 8LD
Ground Capacity: 10,120 (All seats)
Record Attendance: 23,196 (15/11/67)
Pitch Size: 110 × 72 yards

Colours: Red and White striped shirts, Black shorts
Telephone Nº: 0870 899-2005
Ticket Office: 0870 899-1976
Fax Number: (01522) 880020
Web Site: www.redimps.com

GENERAL INFORMATION

Car Parking: Stacey West Car Park (limited parking for £5.00 per car). Also some street parking
Coach Parking: South Common (by the ground)
Nearest Railway Station: Lincoln Central
Club Shop: At the ground
Opening Times: Weekdays 9.00am to 5.00pm and Saturday Matchdays 10.00am to 5.00pm
Telephone Nº: 0870 899-2005
Police Telephone Nº: (01522) 529911

GROUND INFORMATION

Away Supporters' Entrances & Sections:
Lincolnshire Co-operative Stand (seated) – Turnstiles 19-23

ADMISSION INFO (2007/2008 PRICES)

Adult Seating: £13.00 – £18.00
Child Seating: £5.00 – £6.00
Concessionary Seating: £9.00 – £12.00
Note: Prices vary depending on the category of the game and discounts are available for advance ticket purchases
Programme Price: £2.50

DISABLED INFORMATION

Wheelchairs: Limited number of spaces available in the disabled section, adjacent to turnstile 23
Helpers: One helper admitted per disabled person
Prices: Applications for disabled passes must be made to the club. Wheelchair-bound disabled are charged concessionary prices. Helpers are admitted free if the disabled fan has a medium/high level disability allowance
Disabled Toilets: Adjacent to disabled area
Contact: (01522) 880011 (Bookings are necessary)

Travelling Supporters' Information:
Routes: From the East: Take the A46 or A158 into the City Centre following Newark (A46) signs into the High Street and take next left (Scorer Street and Cross Street) for the ground; From the North and West: Take the A15 or A57 into the City Centre, then as from the East; From the South: Take the A1 then A46 for the City Centre, then into the High Street, parking on the South Common or in the Stadium via South Park Avenue, turn down by the Fire Station.

LIVERPOOL FC

Founded: 1892 (**Entered League:** 1893)
Nickname: 'Reds'
Ground: Anfield Road, Liverpool   L4 0TH
Ground Capacity: 45,362 (All seats)
Record Attendance: 61,905 (2/2/52)
Pitch Size: 111 × 74 yards

Colours: Red shirts, shorts and socks
Telephone N°: (0151) 263-2361
Ticket Office: 0844 844-0844
Ticket Office Fax Number: (0151) 261-1416
Customer Services: 0844 844-2005
General Fax Number: (0151) 260-8813
Web Site: www.liverpoolfc.tv

GENERAL INFORMATION

Car Parking: Stanley Park car park (Permit holders only)
Coach Parking: Priory Road and Pinehurst Avenue
Nearest Railway Station: Kirkdale (¾ mile)
Nearest Bus Station: Paradise Street, Liverpool
Club Shop: At the ground and also at Williamson Square in the City Centre and in Chester City Centre
Opening Times: At Anfield: Monday to Friday 9.30am to 5.00pm, Saturdays 9.30am to 4.00pm; At Williamson Square and Chester: Monday to Friday 9.00am to 5.30pm
Telephone N°: (0151) 263-2361

GROUND INFORMATION

Away Supporters' Entrances & Sections:
Anfield Road

ADMISSION INFO (2007/2008 PRICES)

Adult Seating: £34.00 – £36.00
Adult Kop Seating: £32.00 – £34.00
Senior Citizen Seating: £25.50 – £27.00
Senior Citizen Kop Seating: £24.00 – £25.50
Note: Combined Adult/Child tickets are also available
Programme Price: £3.00

DISABLED INFORMATION

Wheelchairs: 79 spaces available in total in the Paddock Enclosure, Kop Stand and Anfield Road Stand
Helpers: One helper admitted per wheelchair
Prices: £24.00 – £27.00 the disabled. Helpers are admitted free of charge
Disabled Toilets: Two available in the Paddock, two in the Kop Stand and one in the Anfield Road Stand
Commentaries are available for the visually impaired on request
Contact: 0844 844-2005   (Bookings are necessary)

Travelling Supporters' Information:
Routes: From the North: Exit the M6 at Junction 28 and follow Liverpool A580 signs into Walton Hall Avenue, pass Stanley Park and turn left into Anfield Road; From the South and East: Take the M62 to the end of the motorway, then turn right into Queen's Drive (A5058) and turn left after 3 miles into Utting Avenue. After 1 mile, turn right into Anfield Road; From North Wales: Take the Mersey Tunnel into the City Centre and follow signs for Preston (A580) into Walton Hall Avenue. Turn right into Anfield Road before Stanley Park.

LUTON TOWN FC

Founded: 1885 (**Entered League**: 1897)
Former Names: The club was formed by the amalgamation of Wanderers FC and Excelsior FC
Nickname: 'Hatters'
Ground: Kenilworth Road Stadium, 1 Maple Road, Luton   LU4 8AW
Ground Capacity: 10,226 (All seats)
Record Attendance: 30,069 (4/3/59)

Pitch Size: 110 × 72 yards
Colours: Shirts are White with Black trim, Black shorts
Telephone Nº: (01582) 411622
Ticket Office: (01582) 416976
Fax Number: (01582) 405070
Web Site: www.lutontown.co.uk

GENERAL INFORMATION
Car Parking: Street parking
Coach Parking: Luton Bus Station
Nearest Railway Station: Luton (1 mile)
Nearest Bus Station: Bute Street, Luton
Club Shop: Kenilworth Road Forecourt
Opening Times: 10.00am to 4.00pm
Telephone Nº: (01582) 411622
Police Telephone Nº: (01582) 401212

GROUND INFORMATION
Away Supporters' Entrances & Sections:
Oak Road for the Oak Stand

ADMISSION INFO (2007/2008 PRICES)
Adult Seating: £15.00 – £26.00
Senior Citizen/Child Seating: £9.00 – £12.00
Note: Tickets are cheaper if bought prior to the matchday
Programme Price: £3.00

DISABLED INFORMATION
Wheelchairs: 32 spaces in total for Home and Away fans in the disabled section, Kenilworth Road End and Main Stand
Helpers: One helper admitted per disabled person
Prices: £11.00 for the disabled. Free of charge for helpers
Disabled Toilets: Available adjacent to disabled area
Commentaries are available for the blind
Contact: (01582) 416976   (Bookings are necessary)

Travelling Supporters' Information:
Routes: From the North and West: Exit the M1 at Junction 11 and follow signs for Luton (A505) into Dunstable Road. Follow the one-way system and turn right back towards Dunstable, take the second left into Ash Road for the ground; From the South and East: Exit the M1 at Junction 10 (or A6/A612) into Luton Town Centre and follow signs into Dunstable Road. After the railway bridge, take the sixth turning on the left into Ash Road for the ground.

MACCLESFIELD TOWN FC

Founded: 1874 (**Entered League:** 1997)
Former Names: Macclesfield FC
Nickname: 'The Silkmen'
Ground: Moss Rose Ground, London Road, Macclesfield, Cheshire   SK11 7SP
Ground Capacity: 6,141
Seating Capacity: 2,520
Record Attendance: 10,041 (1948)

Pitch Size: 110 × 72 yards
Colours: Blue shirts and White shorts
Telephone Nº: (01625) 264686
Ticket Office: (01625) 264686
Fax Number: (01625) 264692
Web Site: www.mtfc.co.uk

GENERAL INFORMATION

Car Parking: Ample parking available near the ground
Coach Parking: Near the ground
Nearest Railway Station: Macclesfield (1 mile)
Nearest Bus Station: Macclesfield
Club Shop: At the ground
Opening Times: Weekdays and matchdays 9.00am to 5.00pm
Telephone Nº: (01625) 264686
Police Telephone Nº: (01625) 610000

GROUND INFORMATION

Away Supporters' Entrances & Sections:
Silkman Terrace and the left side of the McAlpine Stand

ADMISSION INFO (2007/2008 PRICES)

Adult Standing: £10.00
Adult Seating: £13.00
Child/Senior Citizen Standing: £7.00
Child/Senior Citizen Seating: £5.00 – £10.00
Adult Hospitality Package: £32.50
Programme Price: £2.00

DISABLED INFORMATION

Wheelchairs: 45 spaces in front of the Estate Road Stand
Helpers: One helper admitted per disabled fan
Prices: Concessionary prices apply for disabled and helpers
Disabled Toilets: 3 available
Contact: (01625) 264686   (Bookings are necessary)

Travelling Supporters' Information:
Routes: From the North: Exit the M6 at Junction 19 to Knutsford, follow the A537 to Macclesfield. Follow signs for the Town Centre, then for the A523 to Leek. The ground is 1 mile out of the Town Centre on the right; From the South: Exit M6 at Junction 17 for Sandbach and follow the A534 to Congleton. Then take the A536 to Macclesfield. After passing The Rising Sun on the left, ¼ mile further on turn right after the Texaco Garage (Moss Lane). Following this lane will bring you back to the ground.

MANCHESTER CITY FC

Founded: 1887 (**Entered League:** 1892)
Former Name: Ardwick FC (1887-1894)
Nickname: 'Citizens' 'City' 'Blues'
Ground: City of Manchester Stadium, SportCity, Manchester M11 3FF
Ground Capacity: 47,200 (All seats)
Record Attendance: 47,304 (vs Chelsea – 2004)
Pitch Size: 115 × 75 yards

Colours: Sky Blue shirts with White shorts
Telephone Nº: 0870 062-1894
Ticket Office: 0870 062-1894
Credit Card Bookings: 0870 062-1894
Fax Number: (0161) 438-7999
Web Site: www.mcfc.co.uk

GENERAL INFORMATION

Car Parking: 1,000 spaces available at the stadium. Another 7,000 spaces are available off site in the vicinity.
Coach Parking: Around 40 spaces available at the stadium
Nearest Railway Station: Ashburys (15 minutes walk) or Manchester Piccadilly (20 minutes walk)
Nearest Bus Station: 53, 54, 185, 216, 217, 230, 231, 232, 233, 234, 235, 236, 137, X36, X37 services all stop at the stadium
Club Shop: At the stadium
Opening Times: Monday to Saturday 9.00am – 5.00pm, Matchdays 9.00am – 6.00pm, Sundays 11.00am – 4.00pm
Telephone Nº: 0870 062-1894
Police Telephone Nº: (0161) 872-5050

GROUND INFORMATION

Away Supporters' Entrances & Sections: South Stand

ADMISSION INFO (2007/2008 PRICES)

Adult Seating: £23.00 – £38.00
Child Seating: £10.00
Senior Citizen Seating: £11.00 – £22.00
Note: Prices vary depending on the category of the game and discounts are available for tickets purchased in advance
Programme Price: £3.00

DISABLED INFORMATION

Wheelchairs: Around 200 spaces available in total
Helpers: One helper admitted per wheelchair
Prices: £14.00 – £21.00 per disabled fan
Disabled Toilets: Available in all stands
Commentaries for the blind and lifts are also available
Contact: (0161) 438-7747 (Bookings are recommended)

Travelling Supporters' Information:
Routes: From the North: Exit the M60 at Junction 23 onto the A662 Ashton New Road. The stadium is approximately 1½ miles on the right hand side; From the East: Take the A635 which becomes the A662 Ashton New Road. Then as from the North; From the South: Take the M56 onto the M60. Join the A34 Kingsway at Junction 3. Follow the A34 until you join the A6010 Alan Turing Way. The Stadium is situated on the left, after approximately 2½ miles; From the West: Take the M61 to the M60. Exit at Junction 23, then follow directions as from the North.

MANCHESTER UNITED FC

Founded: 1878 (**Entered League:** 1892)
Former Names: Newton Heath LYR FC (1878-1892), Newton Heath FC (1892-1902)
Nickname: 'Red Devils'
Ground: Sir Matt Busby Way, Old Trafford, Manchester M16 0RA
Ground Capacity: 76,312 (All seats)
Record Attendance: 76,962 (25/3/39)

Pitch Size: 115 × 76 yards
Colours: Red shirts with White shorts
Telephone Nº: (0161) 868-8000
Ticket Information: (0870) 757-1968
Fax Number: (0161) 868-8804
Web Site: www.manutd.com

GENERAL INFORMATION

Car Parking: Lancashire Cricket Ground and Car Park E3 on John Gilbert Way. Other approved car parks are signposted
Coach Parking: By Police direction
Nearest Railway Station: At the ground
Nearest Bus Station: Chorlton Street
Nearest Metro Station: Old Trafford, located at L.C.C.C. and also Salford Quays
Club Shop: At the ground
Opening Times: Weekdays 9.00am – 5.30pm; Matchdays 9.00am to kick-off + 1 hour after match; Sundays 10.30am – 4.30pm; Non-match Saturdays 9.00am – 5.00pm
Telephone Nº: (0161) 868-8000
Museum & Tour Centre: (0161) 868-8631
Police Telephone Nº: (0161) 872-5050

GROUND INFORMATION

Away Supporters' Entrances & Sections:
South Stand (turnstile 22) & East Stand (turnstile 30)

ADMISSION INFO (2007/2008 PRICES)

Adult Seating: £25.00 – £44.00
Senior Citizen Seating: £12.50 – £21.00
Under-16s Seating: £10.00
Programme Price: £3.00

DISABLED INFORMATION

Wheelchairs: 104 spaces in total for Home and Away fans in the disabled section – in front of 'L' Stand
Helpers: One helper admitted per disabled person
Prices: Free of charge for the disabled and helpers
Disabled Toilets: Located near the disabled section
Commentaries are available for the visually impaired
Contact: (0161) 868-8000 (Bookings are necessary)

Travelling Supporters' Information:
Routes: From the North and West: Take the M61 to the M60 and exit at Junction 4 following Manchester (A5081) signs. Turn right after 2½ miles into Sir Matt Busby Way for the ground; From the South: Exit the M6 at Junction 19 and take Stockport (A556) road then Altrincham (A56). From Altrincham follow Manchester signs and turn left into Sir Matt Busby Way after 6 miles; From the East: Exit the M62 at Junction 17 and take the A56 to Manchester. Follow signs for the South then signs for Chester (Chester Road). Turn right into Sir Matt Busby Way after 2 miles.

MANSFIELD TOWN FC

Founded: 1897 (**Entered League:** 1931)
Former Name: Mansfield Wesleyans FC (1897-1905)
Nickname: 'Stags'
Ground: Field Mill Ground, Quarry Lane, Mansfield, Nottinghamshire NG18 5DA
Ground Capacity: 10,000 (All seats)
Record Attendance: 24,467 (10/1/53)
Pitch Size: 114 × 70 yards

Colours: Amber shirts with Royal Blue piping, Royal Blue shorts with Amber flash
Telephone Nº: (0870) 756-3160
Ticket Office: (0870) 756-3160
Fax Number: (01623) 482495
Web Site: www.mansfieldtown.net

GENERAL INFORMATION

Car Parking: Large car park at the ground
Coach Parking: Adjacent to the ground
Nearest Railway Station: Mansfield (5 minutes walk)
Nearest Bus Station: Mansfield
Club Shop: At the ground
Opening Times: Weekdays 9.00am – 5.00pm and Matchdays 10.00am – 3.00pm and 4.30pm – 5.30pm
Telephone Nº: (0870) 756-3160
Police Telephone Nº: (01623) 420999

GROUND INFORMATION

Away Supporters' Entrances & Sections:
North Stand turnstiles for North Stand seating

ADMISSION INFO (2007/2008 PRICES)

Adult Seating: £15.00 – £16.00 (Away fans £16.00)
Senior Citizen Seating: £10.00 – £11.00 (Away £10.00)
Junior Seating: £7.00 – £8.00
Under-10s Seating: £5.00 (in the Family Stand only)
Programme Price: £2.50

DISABLED INFORMATION

Wheelchairs: 90 spaces available in total in the disabled sections in the North Stand, Quarry Street Stand & West Stand
Helpers: Admitted
Prices: £8.00 for the disabled. Helpers £15.00
Disabled Toilets: Available in the North Stand, West Stand and Quarry Lane Stand
Contact: (0870) 756-3160 (Please buy tickets in advance)

Travelling Supporters' Information:
Routes: From the North: Exit the M1 at Junction 29 and take the A617 to Mansfield. After 6¼ miles turn right at the Leisure Centre into Rosemary Street. Carry on to Quarry Lane and turn right; From the South and West: Exit the M1 at Junction 28 and take the A38 to Mansfield. After 6½ miles turn right at the crossroads into Belvedere Street then turn right after ¼ mile into Quarry Lane; From the East: Take the A617 to Rainworth, turn left at the crossroads after 3 miles into Windsor Road and turn right at the end into Nottingham Road, then left into Quarry Lane.

MIDDLESBROUGH FC

Founded: 1876 (**Entered League**: 1899)
Nickname: 'Boro'
Ground: Riverside Stadium, Middlesbrough, TS3 6RS
Ground Capacity: 35,100 (All seats)
Record Attendance: 34,836 (28th December 2004)
Pitch Size: 115 × 75 yards

Colours: Red shirts and shorts
Telephone Nº: 0844 499-6789
Ticket Office: 0844 499-1234
Fax Number: (01642) 757690
Web Site: www.mfc.co.uk

GENERAL INFORMATION

Car Parking: 1,250 spaces (Season Car Park passes only)
Coach Parking: At the ground
Nearest Railway Station: Middlesbrough (½ mile)
Nearest Bus Station: Middlesbrough
Club Shops: At ground and Captain Cook Square
Opening Times: Weekdays 9.30am – 5.00pm and Saturday Matchdays 9.30am until kick-off;   Captain Cook Square: Monday to Saturday 9.00am – 5.30pm
Telephone Nº: 0844 499-2676 (Ground);
(01642) 877849 (Captain Cook Square)
Police Telephone Nº: (01642) 248184

GROUND INFORMATION

Away Supporters' Entrances & Sections:
South Stand turnstiles for the South Stand

ADMISSION INFO (2007/2008 PRICES)

Adult Seating: £23.00 – £39.00
Child/Senior Citizen Seating: £14.00 – £26.00
Note: Prices vary depending on the category of the game and the area of the ground
Programme Price: £3.00

DISABLED INFORMATION

Wheelchairs: 170 spaces in total for home and away fans in the disabled areas in the West and South Stands
Helpers: One helper admitted per disabled person
Prices: Disabled and helpers pay half normal prices
Disabled Toilets: Available in the West and South Stands
Contact: 0844 499-1234   (Bookings are necessary)
E-mail contact: disability@mfc.co.uk

Travelling Supporters' Information:
Routes: From the North: Take the A19 across the flyover and join the A66 (Eastbound). At the end of the flyover, turn left at North Ormesby roundabout. The ground is 200 metres down the road; From the South: Take the A1 and A19 to the junction with the A66 (Eastbound). After the flyover, turn left at the North Ormesby roundabout for the ground.

MILLWALL FC

Founded: 1885 (**Entered League**: 1920)
Former Names: Millwall Rovers FC (1885-1893);
Millwall Athletic FC (1893-1925)
Nickname: 'Lions'
Ground: The Den, Zampa Road, London SE16 3LN
Ground Capacity: 20,146 (All seats)
Record Attendance: 20,093 (10/1/94)

Pitch Size: 115 × 74 yards
Colours: Blue shirts with White shorts
Telephone Nº: (020) 7232-1222
Ticket Office: (020) 7231-9999
Fax Number: (020) 7231-3663
Web Site: www.millwallfc.co.uk

GENERAL INFORMATION

Car Parking: Street parking
Coach Parking: Adjacent to the ground
Nearest Railway Station: New Cross Gate (1 mile) or
South Bermondsey (½ mile)
Nearest Tube: New Cross Gate (1 mile)/Surrey Quays (1 mile)
Club Shop: Next to the Stadium
Opening Times: Daily 9.30am to 4.30pm
Telephone Nº: (020) 7231-9845
Police Telephone Nº: (020) 7679-9217

GROUND INFORMATION

Away Supporters' Entrances & Sections:
North Stand turnstiles 31-36

ADMISSION INFO (2007/2008 PRICES)

Adult Seating: £20.00 – £27.00
Child Seating: £7.00 – £12.00
Concessionary Seating: £13.00 – £17.00
Note: Discounts are available for advance purchases
Programme Price: £3.00

DISABLED INFORMATION

Wheelchairs: 78 spaces in the disabled section in the West
Stand and a new area is available with 17 spaces for away
fans in front of the North Stand
Helpers: One helper admitted per wheelchair disabled
Prices: Standard prices for the disabled. Free for helpers
Disabled Toilets: 17 toilets available around the Stadium
Commentaries are available for the blind
Contact: (020) 7232-1222 (Bookings are necessary)

Travelling Supporters' Information:
Routes: From the North: Follow City signs from the M1/A1 then signs for Shoreditch & Whitechapel. Follow Ring Road signs for Dover, cross over Tower Bridge and after 1 mile take 1st exit at the roundabout onto the A2. From Elephant and Castle take the A2 (New Kent Road) into Old Kent Road and turn left after 4 miles at Canterbury Arms pub into Ilderton Road to Zampa Road; From the South: Take the A20 & A21 following signs to London. At New Cross follow signs for Surrey Quays into Kender Street, turn left into Old Kent Road then right into Ilderton Road. Zampa Road is the 7th turning on the right; From the East: Take the A2 to New Cross (then as from the South); From the West: From M4 & M3 follow the South Circular (A205) then follow signs for Clapham, the City (A3) then Camberwell to New Cross and then as from South.

MILTON KEYNES DONS FC

Founded: 1889 (**Entered League**: 1977)
Former Name: Wimbledon Old Centrals FC (1889-1905); Wimbledon FC (1905-2004)
Nickname: 'Dons'
Ground: Stadium:MK, Stadium Way West, Milton Keynes   MK1 1FA
Ground Capacity: 30,000 (All seats)

Pitch Size: 110 × 74 yards
Colours: White with Black and Gold trim
Telephone Nº: (01908) 607090
Ticket Office: (01908) 609000
Fax Number: (01908) 209449
Web Site: www.mkdons.com

GENERAL INFORMATION

Car Parking: 2,000 Pay and Display spaces nearby
Coach Parking: By Police direction
Nearest Railway Station: Bletchley (½ mile)
Nearest Bus Station: Milton Keynes
Club Shop: At the Stadium
Opening Times: Weekdays 10.00amto 5.00pm with extended hours on Matchdays
Telephone Nº: (01908) 209455
Police Telephone Nº: (01908) 686001

GROUND INFORMATION

Away Supporters' Entrances & Sections: North Stand corner

ADMISSION INFO (2007/2008 PRICES)

Adult Seating: £15.00 – £35.00
Child/Senior Citizen Seating: £11.00 – £30.00
Junior Members Seating: £5.00 – £25.00
Programme Price: £2.50

DISABLED INFORMATION

Wheelchairs: Accommodated around the ground
Helpers: One helper admitted per disabled person
Prices: Concessionary prices for the disabled. Helpers are admitted free of charge
Disabled Toilets: Available
Contact: (01908) 609000 (Book 1 month in advance)

Travelling Supporters' Information:
Routes: From all parts: Exit the M1 at Junction 14, following signs for Milton Keynes and cross the first roundabout onto H6 Childs Way. Turn left at the next roundabout onto V11 Tongwell Street. Continue along this road then turn right at the third roundabout onto H9 Groveway. Continue along Groveway then take the first exit at the fourth roundabout towards Central Bletchley. Stadium:MK is the first turning on the left.

MORECAMBE FC

Founded: 1920 (**Entered League:** 2007)
Former Names: None
Nickname: 'Shrimps'
Ground: Christie Park, Lancaster Road, Morecambe, LA4 5TJ
Record Attendance: 9,324 (1962)
Pitch Size: 118 × 76 yards

Colours: Red shirts with White shorts
Telephone Nº: (01524) 411797
Daytime Phone Nº: (01524) 411797
Fax Number: (01524) 832230
Ground Capacity: 6,300
Seating Capacity: 1,200
Web site: www.morecambefc.com

GENERAL INFORMATION
Supporters Club: c/o Club
Telephone Nº: –
Car Parking: At the ground
Coach Parking: At the ground
Nearest Railway Station: Morecambe Central (½ mile)
Nearest Bus Station: Morecambe
Club Shop: At the ground
Opening Times: Weekdays & Matchdays 9.00am to 5.00pm
Telephone Nº: (01524) 411797
Police Telephone Nº: (01524) 411534

GROUND INFORMATION
Away Supporters' Entrances & Sections:
Entrances at the corner of the South Terrace and Lancaster Road for South Terrace accommodation (when segregated)

ADMISSION INFO (2007/2008 PRICES)
Adult Standing: £13.00
Adult Seating: £14.00
Child Standing: £4.00
Child Seating: £5.00
Senior Citizen Standing: £10.00
Senior Citizen Seating: £11.00
Programme Price: £2.50

DISABLED INFORMATION
Wheelchairs: 18 spaces available in the Disabled Stand and 20 spaces are available in the North Stand
Helpers: Admitted
Prices: Concessionary prices are charged
Disabled Toilets: Available in the North Stand
Contact: (01524) 411797 (Bookings are preferred)

Travelling Supporters' Information:
Routes: Exit the M6 at Junction 34. Then take the A683 west in Lancaster and pick up the A589 to Morecambe. At the 2nd roundabout on the outskirts of Morecambe, take the 2nd exit into Lancaster Road and the ground is on the left, approximately 800 yards.

NEWCASTLE UNITED FC

Founded: 1882 (**Entered League**: 1893)
Former Names: Newcastle East End FC (1882-1892) amalgamated with Newcastle West End FC
Nickname: 'Magpies'
Ground: St. James' Park, Newcastle-Upon-Tyne, NE1 4ST
Ground Capacity: 52,387 (All seats)
Record Attendance: 68,386 (3/9/30)

Pitch Size: 115 × 74 yards
Colours: Black and White striped shirts, Black shorts
Telephone Nº: (0191) 201-8400
Ticket Office: (0191) 261-1571
Fax Number: (0191) 201-8600
Web Site: www.nufc.co.uk

GENERAL INFORMATION
Car Parking: Street parking
Coach Parking: By Police direction
Nearest Railway Station: Newcastle Central (¼ mile)
Nearest Bus Station: Gallowgate (¼ mile)
Club Shop: At Ground, Eldon Way, MetroCentre & Monument
Opening Times: All shops are open Monday to Saturday 9.00am – 5.00pm; Eldon open until 8.00pm on Thursdays; MetroCentre open until at least 7.00pm Monday to Saturday; Monument Mall open to 8pm Thursdays & 6pm Saturdays
Telephone Nº: (0191) 201-8426

GROUND INFORMATION
Away Supporters' Entrances & Sections: North West Corner of Sir John Hall Stand, entrance from Barrack Road

ADMISSION INFO (2007/2008 PRICES)
Adult Seating: £20.00 – £35.00
Child Seating: £7.00 – £17.00
Senior Citizen Seating: £17.00 – £28.00
Programme Price: £3.00

DISABLED INFORMATION
Wheelchairs: 103 spaces in total in the disabled areas, Sir John Hall Stand and Newcastle Brown Stand
Helpers: One helper admitted per disabled person
Prices: Prices available on application
Disabled Toilets: Available in the Newcastle Brown and Sir John Hall Stands.
Commentaries are available for 20 blind supporters
Contact: (0191) 261-1571 (Bookings are necessary)

Travelling Supporters' Information:
Routes: From the North: Follow the A1 into Newcastle, then follow Hexham signs into Percy Street. Turn right into Leazes Park Road; From the South: Take the A1M, then after Birtley Granada Services take the A1 Gateshead Western Bypass (bear left on the Motorway). Follow Airport signs for approximately 3 miles then take the A692 (Newcastle) sign, crossing the Redheugh Bridge. Proceed over three sets of traffic lights to the roundabout and take the 1st exit into Barrack Road; From the West: Take the A69 towards the City Centre. Pass Newcastle General Hospital. At the traffic lights after the Hospital turn left into Brighton Grove. After 70 yards turn right into Stanhope Street and proceed into Barrack Road for the ground.

NORTHAMPTON TOWN FC

Founded: 1897 (**Entered League:** 1920)
Nickname: 'Cobblers'
Ground: Sixfields Stadium, Upton Way, Northampton NN5 5QA
Ground Capacity: 7,653 (All seats)
Record Attendance: 7,557 (26/9/98)
Pitch Size: 116 × 72 yards

Colours: Claret and White shirts with White shorts
Telephone Nº: (01604) 757773
Ticket Office: (01604) 588338
Fax Number: (01604) 751613
Web Site: www.ntfc.co.uk

GENERAL INFORMATION

Car Parking: At the ground
Coach Parking: At the ground
Nearest Railway Station: Northampton Castle (2 miles)
Nearest Bus Station: Greyfriars
Club Shop: At the ground
Opening Times: Monday to Thursday 10.00am – 5.00pm, Friday 10.00am – 7.00pm, non-match Saturdays 10.00am – 12.00pm and Matchdays 10.00am to kick-off and 30 minutes after the final whistle
Telephone Nº: (0870) 011-7773
Police Telephone Nº: (01604) 700700

GROUND INFORMATION

Away Supporters' Entrances & Sections:
Paul Cox Panel & Paint Stand

ADMISSION INFO (2007/2008 PRICES)

Adult Seating: £16.00 – £19.00
Senior Citizen Seating: £11.50 – £13.50
Under-16s Seating: £5.50 – £12.00
Under-7s: Admitted free of charge
Note: A range of concessionary prices are available
Programme Price: £2.00

DISABLED INFORMATION

Wheelchairs: 80 spaces in total for Home and Away fans in various areas of the ground
Helpers: One helper admitted per disabled person
Prices: Please contact the club for details
Disabled Toilets: Available by the disabled areas
Commentaries are available for the blind
Contact: (01604) 588338 (Bookings are necessary)

Travelling Supporters' Information:
Routes: From All Parts: Exit the M1 at Junction 15A following the signs for Sixfields Leisure onto Upton Way – the ground is approximately 2 miles.

NORWICH CITY FC

Founded: 1902 (**Entered League:** 1920)
Nickname: 'Canaries'
Ground: Carrow Road, Norwich   NR1 1JE
Ground Capacity: 26,034 (All seats)
Record Attendance: 43,984 (30/3/63)
Pitch Size: 114 × 74 yards

Colours: Yellow shirts with Green shorts
Telephone N°: (01603) 760760
Ticket Office: (0870) 444-1902
Fax Number: (01603) 613886
Web Site: www.canaries.co.uk

GENERAL INFORMATION

Car Parking: City Centre car parks (nearby)
Coach Parking: Lower Clarence Road
Nearest Railway Station: Norwich Thorpe (1 mile)
Nearest Bus Station: Surrey Street, Norwich
Club Shop: In the Geoffrey Watling City Stand
Opening Times: Weekdays & Matchdays 9.00am to 5.00pm
Telephone N°: (01603) 218711
Police Telephone N°: (01603) 768769

GROUND INFORMATION

Away Supporters' Entrances & Sections:
Jarrold Stand usings turnstiles 51-57

ADMISSION INFO (2007/2008 PRICES)

Adult Seating: £12.00 – £31.00
Concessions & Under 16's Seating: £1.00 – £19.00
Under 12's Seating: £1.00 – £12.00
Programme Price: £3.00
Note: Prices vary according to category of game, the area of the ground and discounts which may be available

DISABLED INFORMATION

Wheelchairs: 74 spaces for home fans and 15 for away fans in Norwich Union Community Stand. Plenty of spaces available for ambulant disabled fans also
Helpers: One helper admitted per disabled person
Prices: A single concessionary price is charged for each disabled fan and helper
Disabled Toilets: Available within the disabled area
Contact: (0870) 444-1902 (Bookings are necessary)

Travelling Supporters' Information:
Routes: From the South: Take the A11 or A140 and turn right onto the A47 towards Great Yarmouth & Lowestoft, take the A146 Norwich/Lowestoft sliproad, turn left towards Norwich and follow road signs for the Football Ground; From the West: Take the A47 on to the A146 Norwich/Lowestoft slip road. Turn left towards Norwich, follow the road signs for the Football Ground.

NOTTINGHAM FOREST FC

Founded: 1865 (**Entered League:** 1892)
Nickname: 'The Reds'
Ground: The City Ground, Nottingham   NG2 5FJ
Ground Capacity: 30,602 (All seats)
Record Attendance: 49,946 (28/10/67)
Pitch Size: 112 × 74 yards

Colours: Red shirts with White shorts
Telephone Nº: (0115) 982-4444
Ticket Office: (0871) 226-1980
Fax Number: (0115) 982-4455
Web Site: www.nottinghamforest.co.uk
Club Call Nº: (0904) 064-1174

GENERAL INFORMATION

Car Parking: East car park (300 spaces) and street parking
Coach Parking: East car park, Meadow Lane
Nearest Railway Station: Nottingham Midland (½ mile)
Nearest Bus Station: Victoria Street/Broadmarsh Centre
Club Shop: At the ground
Opening Times: Weekdays 9.00am – 5.00pm; Matchdays 9.00am – kick-off and 30 minutes after the game; Sunday matchdays 10.00am – kick-off + 30 minutes after the game
Telephone Nº: (0115) 982-4447
Police Telephone Nº: (0115) 948-1888

GROUND INFORMATION

Away Supporters' Entrances & Sections:
Entrances via East car park for Bridgford Stand

ADMISSION INFO (2006/2007 PRICES)

Adult Seating: £22.00 – £26.00
Under-18s: £10.00
Under-12s: £5.00
Concessionary Seating: £17.00 – £20.00
Note: Discounts are available for tickets purchased in advance
Programme Price: £2.50

DISABLED INFORMATION

Wheelchairs: 50 spaces in total for Home and Away fans in the disabled area, in front of Executive Stand
Helpers: One helper admitted per disabled person
Prices: £5.00 for wheelchair disabled. £10.00 for helpers and ambulant disabled
Disabled Toilets: Available in the Executive Stand
Contact: (0115) 982-4445   (Bookings are necessary)

Travelling Supporters' Information:
Routes: From the North: Exit the M1 at Junction 26 following Nottingham signs (A610) then signs to Melton Mowbray and Trent Bridge (A606). Cross the River Trent, turn left into Radcliffe Road then left again into Colwick Road for the ground; From the South: Exit the M1 at Junction 24 following signs for Nottingham (South) to Trent Bridge. Turn right into Radcliffe Road then left into Colwick Road; From the East: Take the A52 to West Bridgford and turn right into Colwick Road; From the West: Take the A52 into Nottingham following signs for Melton Mowbray and Trent Bridge, cross the River Trent (then as from the North).

NOTTS COUNTY FC

Founded: 1862 (**Entered League**: 1888)
Nickname: 'Magpies'
Ground: Meadow Lane, Nottingham NG2 3HJ
Ground Capacity: 20,300 (All seats)
Record Attendance: 47,310 (12/3/55)
Pitch Size: 113 × 72 yards

Colours: Black and White striped shirts, Black shorts
Telephone Nº: (0115) 952-9000
Ticket Office: (0115) 955-7204 (weekdays),
(0115) 955-7210 (matchdays)
Fax Number: (0115) 955-3994
Web Site: www.nottscountyfc.co.uk

GENERAL INFORMATION

Car Parking: British Waterways, Meadow Lane
Coach Parking: Incinerator Road (Cattle Market Corner)
Nearest Railway Station: Nottingham Midland (½ mile)
Nearest Bus Station: Broadmarsh Centre
Club Shop: At the ground
Opening Times: Closed Mondays; Tuesday to Friday
9.00am – 5.00pm, Saturday Matchdays 9.30am – 5.30pm,
other Saturdays 9.00am – 1.00pm
Telephone Nº: (0115) 952-9000
Police Telephone Nº: (0115) 948-1888

GROUND INFORMATION

Away Supporters' Entrances & Sections:
Cattle Market Corner for The Kop Stand

ADMISSION INFO (2007/2008 PRICES)

Adult Seating: £16.00 – £18.00
Child Seating: £5.00 (Under-15s); £9.00 (16-18 years)
Senior Citizens: £10.00 – £11.00
Note: Category A games cost an additional £2.00
Programme Price: £2.50

DISABLED INFORMATION

Wheelchairs: 100 spaces in total in the disabled area,
County Road/Meadow Lane End corner
Helpers: One helper admitted per disabled fan
Prices: 75% of normal prices for the disabled. Helpers are
admitted free of charge
Disabled Toilets: Available next to the disabled area
Contact: (0115) 955-7204 (Bookings are necessary)

Travelling Supporters' Information:
Routes: From the North: Exit the M1 at Junction 26 following Nottingham signs (A610) then Melton Mowbray and Trent Bridge (A606) signs. Before the River Trent turn left into Meadow Lane; From the South: Exit the M1 at Junction 24 following signs for Nottingham (South) to Trent Bridge, cross the river and follow the one-way system to the right, then turn left and right at the traffic lights then second right into Meadow Lane; From the East: Take the A52 to West Bridgford/Trent Bridge, cross the river and follow the one-way system to the right then turn left and right at the traffic lights, then second right into Meadow Lane; From the West: Take the A52 into Nottingham following signs for Melton Mowbray and Trent Bridge. Before the River Trent turn left into Meadow Lane.

OLDHAM ATHLETIC FC

Founded: 1895 (**Entered League:** 1907)
Former Names: Pine Villa FC (1895-1899)
Nickname: 'Latics'
Ground: Boundary Park, Oldham   OL1 2PA
Ground Capacity: 13,559 (All seats)
Record Attendance: 47,671 (25/1/30)
Pitch Size: 110 × 72 yards

Colours: Royal Blue shirts and shorts, White socks
Telephone Nº: (0871) 226-2235
Ticket Office: (0871) 226-2235
Fax Number: (0871) 226-1715
Web Site: www.oldhamathletic.co.uk

GENERAL INFORMATION
Car Parking: Broadway Stand car park (1,000 cars)
Coach Parking: At the ground
Nearest Railway Station: Oldham Werneth (1½ miles)
Nearest Bus Station: Oldham Town Centre (2 miles)
Club Shop: At the ground
Opening Times: Mondays to Fridays 9.00am to 5.00pm.
Saturdays 9.00am to 12.00pm
Telephone Nº: (0871) 226-1679
Police Telephone Nº: (0161) 624-0444

GROUND INFORMATION
Away Supporters' Entrances & Sections:
Rochdale Road Stand

ADMISSION INFO (2007/2008 PRICES)
Adult Seating: £16.00 – £20.00
Senior Citizen/Under-16s Seating: £10.00 – £11.00
Under-12s Seating: £3.00
Note: Discounts are available for tickets purchased in advance
Programme Price: £3.00

DISABLED INFORMATION
Wheelchairs: 60 spaces in the disabled areas –
Broadway Paddock, Chadderton Road Stand and Rochdale
Road Stand
Helpers: One helper admitted per disabled person
Prices: Normal prices for the disabled. Free for helpers
Disabled Toilets: Available in Broadway Paddock and the
Rochdale Road Stand
Contact: (0871) 226-2235   (Bookings are necessary)

Travelling Supporters' Information:
Routes: From All Parts: Exit the M62 at Junction 20 and take the A627M to the junction with the A664. Take the 1st exit at the roundabout onto Broadway, then the 1st right into Hilbre Avenue which leads to the car park at the ground.

PETERBOROUGH UNITED FC

Founded: 1934 (**Entered League**: 1960)
Nickname: 'Posh'
Ground: London Road, Peterborough PE2 8AL
Ground Capacity: 14,330
Seating Capacity: 7,669
Record Attendance: 30,096 (20/2/65)
Pitch Size: 112 × 71 yards

Colours: Blue shirts with White shorts
Telephone Nº: (01733) 563947
Ticket Office: (01733) 563947
Fax Number: (01733) 344140
Web Site: www.theposh.com

GENERAL INFORMATION
Car Parking: At the ground and also adjacent
Coach Parking: In front of the (North) Main Stand
Nearest Railway Station: Peterborough (1 mile)
Nearest Bus Station: Peterborough (1 mile)
Club Shop: At the ground
Opening Times: Matchdays only 1.00pm to 3.00pm
Telephone Nº: (01733) 563947
Police Telephone Nº: (01733) 563232

GROUND INFORMATION
Away Supporters' Entrances & Sections:
Turnstile A, Moys End for Block A Seating

ADMISSION INFO (2007/2008 PRICES)
Adult Standing: £15.00
Adult Seating: £18.00
Senior Citizen Standing/Seating: £12.00
Child Standing: £9.00
Child Seating: £5.00 – £9.00
Note: Under-10s are admitted free in the South Stand
Programme Price: £2.50

DISABLED INFORMATION
Wheelchairs: 40 spaces in total for Home and Away fans in disabled area, right side of South Stand
Helpers: One helper admitted per disabled person
Prices: £12.00 for the disabled. Free of charge for helpers
Disabled Toilets: Available in the South and Main Stands
Contact: (01733) 563947 (Bookings are necessary)

Travelling Supporters' Information:
Routes: From the North and West: Take the A1 then the A47 into the Town Centre and follow Whittlesey signs across the river into London Road; From the East: Take the A47 into the Town Centre (then as from the North); From the South: Take the A1 then the A15 into London Road.

PLYMOUTH ARGYLE FC |

Founded: 1886 **(Entered League:** 1920)
Former Names: Argyle FC (1886-1903)
Nickname: 'Pilgrims' 'Argyle'
Ground: Home Park, Plymouth   PL2 3DQ
Ground Capacity: 20,922
Seating Capacity: 15,684
Record Attendance: 43,596 (10/10/36)

Pitch Size: 112 × 72 yards
Colours: Green shirts and White shorts
Telephone N°: (01752) 562561
Box Office: 0845 338-7232
Fax Number: (01752) 606167
Web Site: www.pafc.co.uk

GENERAL INFORMATION
Car Parking: Car park for 1,000 cars is adjacent
Coach Parking: Central Park Car Park
Nearest Railway Station: Plymouth North Road
Nearest Bus Station: Bretonside, Plymouth
Club Shop: At the ground
Opening Times: Monday to Friday 9.00am – 5.00pm,
Non-match Saturdays 10.00am – 3.00pm, Saturday
Matchdays 9.00am – 3.00pm & Sundays 12.00pm – 3.00pm
Telephone N°: (01752) 562561
Police Telephone N°: (0990) 777444

GROUND INFORMATION
Away Supporters' Entrances & Sections:
Barn Park End turnstiles for covered accommodation

ADMISSION INFO (2007/2008 PRICES)
Adult Standing: £20.00
Adult Seating: £24.00
Child Standing: £6.00
Child Seating: £6.00
Senior Citizen Standing: £16.00
Senior Citizen/Student Seating: £17.00
Note: Discounted prices are available if tickets are bought
before 5.00pm on the day prior to the game
Programme Price: £2.50

DISABLED INFORMATION
Wheelchairs: 60 spaces in total for Home and Away fans in
the disabled section, Devonport End
Helpers: One helper admitted per disabled person
Prices: Normal prices apply for the disabled and helpers
Disabled Toilets: Adjacent to the disabled section
Commentaries are available for the blind
Contact: (01752) 562561   (Bookings are necessary)

Travelling Supporters' Information:
Routes: From All Parts: Take the A38 to Tavistock Road (A386), then branch left following signs for Home Park (A386) and continue for 1¼ miles. The car park for the ground is on the left (signposted Home Park).

PORTSMOUTH FC

Founded: 1898 (**Entered League**: 1920)
Nickname: 'Pompey'
Ground: Fratton Park, 57 Frogmore Road, Portsmouth, Hants PO4 8RA
Ground Capacity: 20,200 (All seats)
Record Attendance: 51,385 (26th February 1949)
Pitch Size: 108 × 71 yards

Colours: Blue shirts with White shorts
Telephone Nº: (023) 9273-1204
Ticket Office: (0871) 230-1898
Fax Number: (023) 9273-4129
Web Site: www.pompeyfc.co.uk
Club Call Nº: (09068) 121182

GENERAL INFORMATION

Car Parking: Street parking
Coach Parking: By Police direction
Nearest Railway Station: Fratton (adjacent)
Nearest Bus Station: –
Club Shop: At the ground
Opening Times: Monday to Friday 9.00am – 5.30pm and Saturdays 9.00am – 4.00pm. Matchday Saturdays shuts between 3.00pm–4.45pm
Telephone Nº: (023) 9273-8358
Police Telephone Nº: (023) 9232-1111

GROUND INFORMATION

Away Supporters' Entrances & Sections:
Aspley Road – Milton Road side for Aspley Road End

ADMISSION INFO (2007/2008 PRICES)

Adult Seating: £32.00 – £37.00
Child Seating: £12.00 – £22.00
Senior Citizen Seating: £19.00 – £27.00
Note: Prices vary depending on the category of the game
Programme Price: £3.00

DISABLED INFORMATION

Wheelchairs: Limited number of spaces available in the disabled section, Fratton End
Helpers: One helper admitted per disabled person
Prices: £15.00 for the disabled. Free of charge for helpers
Disabled Toilets: One available in disabled section
Contact: (023) 9273-1204 (Bookings are necessary)

Travelling Supporters' Information:
Routes: From the North and West: Take the M27 and M275 to the end then take the 2nd exit at the roundabout and after ¼ mile turn right at the 'T' junction into London Road (A2047). After 1¼ miles cross the railway bridge and turn left into Goldsmith Avenue. After ½ mile turn left into Frogmore Road; From the East: Take the A27 following Southsea signs (A2030). Turn left at the roundabout (3 miles) onto the A288, then right into Priory Crescent and next right into Carisbrooke Road for the ground.

PORT VALE FC

Founded: 1876 (**Entered League:** 1892)
Former Names: Burslem Port Vale FC
Nickname: 'Valiants'
Ground: Vale Park, Hamil Road, Burslem,
Stoke-on-Trent   ST6 1AW
Ground Capacity: 18,982 (All seats)
Record Attendance: 49,768 (20/2/60)
Pitch Size: 114 × 75 yards

Colours: White shirts with Black and Gold trim,
Black shorts
Telephone Nº: (01782) 655800
Ticket Office: (01782) 655832
Fax Number: (01782) 834981
Web Site: www.port-vale.co.uk
Club Call Nº: (09068) 121636

GENERAL INFORMATION

Car Parking: Car parks at the ground
Coach Parking: Hamil Road car park
Nearest Railway Station: Stoke
Nearest Bus Station: Burslem (adjacent)
Club Shop: At the ground
Opening Times: Monday to Saturday 9.00am – 5.00pm
Telephone Nº: (01782) 655833
Police Telephone Nº: (0845) 330-2010

GROUND INFORMATION

Away Supporters' Entrances & Sections:
Hamil Road turnstiles for the Phones 4U Stand

ADMISSION INFO (2007/2008 PRICES)

Adult Seating: £19.00
Child Seating: £8.00
Young Adult (up to the Age of 21) Seating: £12.20
Senior Citizen Seating: £12.50
Note: Family tickets are also available
Programme Price: £2.50

DISABLED INFORMATION

Wheelchairs: 20 spaces available in the Disabled Stand,
Lorne Street/Bycars Corner
Helpers: One helper admitted per disabled person
Prices: £6.50 each for disabled fan. £12.50 for helpers
Disabled Toilets: Available in the disabled area
Commentaries are available – please contact the club
Contact: (01782) 655800   (Bookings are necessary)

Travelling Supporters' Information:
Routes: From the North: Exit the M6 at Junction 16 and follow Stoke signs (A500). Branch left off the A500 at the exit signposted Tunstall and take the 2nd exit at the roundabout into Newcastle Street. Proceed through the traffic lights into Moorland Road and take the 2nd turning on the left into Hamil Road; From the South and West: Exit the M6 at Junction 15 and take the A5006 and A500. After 6¼ miles branch left (then as from the North); From the East: Take the A50 or A52 into Stoke following Burslem signs into Waterloo Road, turn right at Burslem crossroads into Moorland Road (then as from the North).

PRESTON NORTH END FC

Founded: 1881 (**Entered League**: 1888)
Nickname: 'Lilywhites' 'North End'
Ground: Deepdale, Preston   PR1 6RU
Ground Capacity: 21,784 (All seats)
Record Attendance: 42,684 (23/4/38)
Pitch Size: 110 × 72 yards

Colours: White shirts with Blue shorts
Telephone Nº: (0870) 4421964
Ticket Office: (0870) 4421966
Fax Number: (01772) 693366
Web Site: www.pne.com

GENERAL INFORMATION

Car Parking: Sir Tom Finney Car Park, Moor Park and Deepdale Primary School
Coach Parking: Deepdale Retail Park
Nearest Railway Station: Preston (2 miles)
Nearest Bus Station: Preston (1 mile)
Club Shop: At the ground
Opening Times: Monday to Saturday 9.00am to 5.00pm, Sunday 11.00am to 4.00pm
Telephone Nº: (0870) 4421964
Police Telephone Nº: (01772) 203203

GROUND INFORMATION

Away Supporters' Entrances & Sections:
Bill Shankly End

ADMISSION INFO (2007/2008 PRICES)

Adult Seating: £22.00 – £25.00
Child Seating: £6.00 – £8.00 (Under-8s admitted free)
Senior Citizen Seating: £14.00
Note: Tickets are cheaper if bought prior to the matchday
Programme Price: £3.00

DISABLED INFORMATION

Wheelchairs: Spaces available for season ticket holders only
Helpers: One helper admitted per wheelchair
Prices: Concessionary prices for the disabled and helpers
Disabled Toilets: Available in the Tom Finney Stand and the BSK and AK Town End
Commentaries are available for the blind
Contact: (0870) 4421964 (Bookings are usually necessary)

Travelling Supporters' Information:
Routes: From the North: Take the M6 then the M55 to Junction 1. Follow signs for Preston (A6). After 2 miles turn left at the crossroads into Blackpool Road (A5085). Turn right ¾ mile into Deepdale; From the South and East: Exit the M6 at Junction 31 and follow Preston signs (A59). Take the 2nd exit at the roundabout (1 mile) into Blackpool Road. Turn left after 1¼ miles into Deepdale; From the West: Exit the M55 at Junction 1 (then as from the North).

QUEEN'S PARK RANGERS FC

Founded: 1882 (**Entered League**: 1920)
Former Names: Formed by the amalgamation of St. Jude's FC and Christchurch Rangers FC
Nickname: 'Rangers' 'R's'
Ground: Loftus Road Stadium, South Africa Road, London W12 7PA
Ground Capacity: 18,400 (All seats)
Record Attendance: 35,353 (27/4/74)

Pitch Size: 112 × 72 yards
Colours: Blue and White hooped shirts, White shorts
Telephone Nº: (020) 8743-0262
Ticket Office: (0870) 112-1967
Fax Number: (020) 8749-0994
Web Site: www.qpr.co.uk

GENERAL INFORMATION
Car Parking: Street parking
Coach Parking: By Police direction
Nearest Railway Station: Ealing Broadway
Nearest Tube Station: White City (Central)
Club Shop: At the ground
Opening Times: Monday to Friday 9.00am – 5.00pm
Saturdays 9.00am – 1.00pm
Telephone Nº: (020) 8749-6862
Police Telephone Nº: (020) 8741-6212

GROUND INFORMATION
Away Supporters' Entrances & Sections:
South Africa Road turnstiles 13-15 & Ellerslie Road turnstiles 9-12 for School End Stand

ADMISSION INFO (2007/2008 PRICES)
Adult Seating: £20.00 – £25.00
Child Seating: £8.00
Senior Citizen/Student Seating: £12.00 – £15.00
Programme Price: £3.00

DISABLED INFORMATION
Wheelchairs: 13 spaces available in a new disabled section in the School End (Lower) Stand
Helpers: One helper admitted per wheelchair
Prices: £15.00 for the disabled. Free of charge for helpers
Disabled Toilets: Available in Ellerslie Road Stand
Commentaries are available for the blind
Contact: Contact the club in writing. Bookings necessary

Travelling Supporters' Information:
Routes: From the North: Take M1 & M406 North Circular for Neasden, go left after ¾ mile (A404) following signs for Harlesden, Hammersmith, past White City Stadium, right into White City Road and left into South Africa Road; From the South: Take A206 then A3 across Putney Bridge and follow signs to Hammersmith then Oxford (A219) to Shepherd's Bush. Join the A4020 following signs to Acton, turn right (¼ mile) into Loftus Road; From the East: Take the A12, A406 then the A503 to join the Ring Road, follow Oxford signs and join the A40(M), branch left (2 miles) to the M41, take the 3rd exit at the roundabout to the A4020 (then as South); From the West: Take the M4 to Chiswick then the A315 & A402 to Shepherd's Bush, join A4020 (then as South).

READING FC

Founded: 1871 (**Entered League:** 1920)
Former Names: Formed by the amalgamation of Hornets FC (1877) and Earley FC (1889)
Nickname: 'Royals'
Ground: Madejski Stadium, Junction 11 M4, Reading, Berkshire   RG2 0FL
Ground Capacity: 24,200
Record Attendance: 24,107 (3rd December 2004)

Pitch Size: 111 × 74 yards
Colours: Blue and White hooped shirts, Blue shorts
Telephone Nº: (0118) 968-1100
Ticket Office: (0870) 999-1871
Fax Number: (0118) 968-1101
Web Site: www.readingfc.co.uk

GENERAL INFORMATION

Car Parking: 1,800 spaces available at the ground. Also another 2,000 spaces available nearby
Coach Parking: By Police direction (at the ground)
Nearest Railway Station: Reading Central
Nearest Bus Station: Reading
Club Shop: At the ground
Opening Times: Monday to Saturday 9.00am – 5.30pm, Sundays 10.00am – 4.00pm
Telephone Nº: (0118) 968-1234
Police Telephone Nº: (0118) 953-6000

GROUND INFORMATION

Away Supporters' Entrances & Sections:
South Stand entrances and accommodation

ADMISSION INFO (2007/2008 PRICES)

Adult Seating: £28.00 – £41.00
Concessionary Seating: £18.00 – £31.00
Child Seating: £6.00 – £21.00
Note: Prices vary depending on the category of the game
Programme Price: £3.00

DISABLED INFORMATION

Wheelchairs: A total of 128 spaces available for wheelchairs throughout the stadium
Helpers: Yes
Prices: £28.00–£41.00 for each disabled fan and one helper.
Disabled Toilets: One available adjacent to stand
Commentaries for approximately 12 people are available
Contact: (0870) 999-1871 (Bookings are necessary)

Travelling Supporters' Information:
Routes: The stadium is situated just off Junction 11 of the M4 near Reading.

ROCHDALE FC

Founded: 1907 (**Entered League:** 1921)
Former Names: Rochdale Town FC
Nickname: 'The Dale'
Ground: Spotland Stadium, Rochdale   OL11 5DS
Ground Capacity: 10,208
Seating Capacity: 8,310
Record Attendance: 24,231 (10/12/49)

Pitch Size: 114 × 76 yards
Colours: Black and White striped shirts, White shorts
Telephone Nº: 0870 822-1907
Ticket Office: 0870 822-1907
Fax Number: (01706) 648466
Web Site: www.rochdaleafc.co.uk

GENERAL INFORMATION

Car Parking: Street parking only
Coach Parking: By Police direction
Nearest Railway Station: Rochdale (2 miles)
Nearest Bus Station: Town Centre (1 mile)
Club Shop: At the ground
Opening Times: Weekdays and Saturday Matchdays from 9.00am to 5.00pm
Telephone Nº: 0870 822-1969
Police Telephone Nº: (0161) 872-5050

GROUND INFORMATION

Away Supporters' Entrances & Sections:
Turnstiles 11 to 18 for Willbutts Lane

ADMISSION INFO (2007/2008 PRICES)

Adult Standing: £12.00
Adult Seating: £15.00 – £18.00
Child/Senior Citizen Standing: £8.00
Child Seating: £5.00 (Under-12s); £7.00 (Under-16s)
(Only available for accompanied Under-16s in the Family Stand)
Senior Citizen Seating: £8.00 – £1.00
Programme Price: £2.50

DISABLED INFORMATION

Wheelchairs: 24 spaces in total in the disabled sections in the Horners, W.M.G. and Willbutts Lane Stands
Helpers: One helper admitted per disabled person
Prices: Concessionary prices for disabled. Free for helpers
Disabled Toilets: Available adjacent to disabled area
Contact: 0870 822-1969   (Bookings are necessary)

Travelling Supporters' Information:
Routes: From All Parts: Exit the M62 at Junction 20 and take the A627M signposted Rochdale. At the end of this link road, filter left carry on for 400 yards and go straight on at the roundabout into Roche Valley Way signposted Spotland Stadium. At the traffic lights go staight ahead and the ground is on the right after ½ mile.

ROTHERHAM UNITED FC

Founded: 1870 (**Entered League**: 1893)
Former Names: Rotherham Town FC (1870-1896), Thornhill United FC (1884-1905) and Rotherham County FC (1905-1925)
Nickname: 'The Millers'
Ground: Millmoor Ground, Rotherham   S60 1HR
Ground Capacity: 8,287 (All seats)
Record Attendance: 25,170 (13/12/52)

Pitch Size: 110 × 72 yards
Colours: Red shirts with White sleeves, White shorts
Telephone Nº: (01709) 512434
Ticket Office: (0870) 443-1884
Fax Number: (01709) 512762
Web Site: www.themillers.co.uk

GENERAL INFORMATION

Car Parking: Kimberworth Road and Main Street car parks
Coach Parking: By Police direction
Nearest Railway Station: Rotherham Central (½ mile)
Nearest Bus Station: Town Centre (½ mile)
Club Shop: At the ground
Opening Times: Weekdays 9.00am – 5.00pm
Telephone Nº: (01709) 512760
Police Telephone Nº: (01709) 371121

GROUND INFORMATION

Away Supporters' Entrances & Sections:
Millmoor Lane turnstiles for Millmoor Lane/Railway End

ADMISSION INFO (2007/2008 PRICES)

Adult Seating: £20.00 – £22.00
Senior Citizen/Student Seating: £12.00 – £14.00
Child Seating: £5.00 – £12.00 (Price depends on age)
Note: Discounts are available for advance bookings
Programme Price: £2.50

DISABLED INFORMATION

Wheelchairs: 18 spaces for Home fans, 17 spaces for Away fans in the disabled section, Millmoor Lane
Helpers: One helper admitted per disabled person
Prices: Disabled and helpers £14.00 each. Wheelchair disabled are admitted free of charge
Disabled Toilets: Two available in the disabled area
Contact: (01709) 512434   (Bookings are necessary)

Travelling Supporters' Information:
Routes: From the North: Exit M1 at Junction 34, follow Rotherham (A6109) signs to the traffic lights and turn right. The ground is ¼ mile on the right over the railway bridge; From the South & West: Exit M1 at Junction 33, turn right and follow Rotherham signs. Turn left at the roundabout then right at the next roundabout. Follow the dual carriageway to the next roundabout and go straight on. Turn left at the next roundabout and the ground is ¼ mile on the left; From the East: Take A630 into Rotherham following Sheffield signs. At the 3rd roundabout turn left (signposted Masborough) – the ground is then on the right.

SCUNTHORPE UNITED FC

Founded: 1899 (**Entered League**: 1950)
Former Name: Scunthorpe and Lindsey United FC (1899-1912)
Nickname: 'The Iron'
Ground: Glanford Park, Doncaster Road, Scunthorpe, North Lincolnshire DN15 8TD
Ground Capacity: 9,095
Seating Capacity: 6,322

Record Attendance: 8,775 (1/5/89)
Pitch Size: 112 × 72 yards
Colours: Shirts and shorts are Claret with Sky Blue trim
Telephone N°: 0871 221-1899
Ticket Office: 0871 221-1899
Fax Number: (01724) 857986
Web Site: www.scunthorpe-united.co.uk

GENERAL INFORMATION

Car Parking: Spaces for 800 cars at the ground
Coach Parking: At the ground
Nearest Railway Station: Scunthorpe (1½ miles)
Nearest Bus Station: Scunthorpe (1½ miles)
Club Shop: At the ground
Opening Times: Weekdays 9.00am to 5.00pm
Matchdays 10.00am to 3.00pm and 4.45pm to 5.15pm
Telephone N°: (01724) 747670
Police Telephone N°: (01724) 282888

GROUND INFORMATION

Away Supporters' Entrances & Sections:
Turnstiles 6-7 for the AMS Stand

ADMISSION INFO (2007/2008 PRICES)

Adult Standing: £15.00 – £16.00
Adult Seating: £18.00 – £28.00
Child Standing: £6.00 – £7.00
Child Seating: £11.00 – £16.00
Programme Price: £2.50

DISABLED INFORMATION

Wheelchairs: 10 spaces for Home fans and 6 spaces for Away fans in the disabled section, Grove Wharf Stand
Helpers: One helper admitted per disabled person
Prices: Free for the disabled. Helpers £9.00
Disabled Toilets: One available in the disabled area
Commentaries are available for the blind
Contact: (01724) 747670 (Bookings are necessary)

Travelling Supporters' Information:
Routes: From All Parts: Exit the M180 at Junction 3 onto the M181. Follow the M181 to the roundabout with the A18 and take the A18 towards Scunthorpe – the ground is on the right after 200 yards.

SHEFFIELD UNITED FC

Founded: 1889 (**Entered League**: 1892)
Nickname: 'Blades'
Ground: Bramall Lane, Sheffield   S2 4SU
Ground Capacity: 32,609 (All seats)
Record Attendance: 68,287 (15/2/36)
Pitch Size: 112 × 72 yards

Colours: Red and White striped shirts, Black shorts
Telephone Nº: 0870 787-1960
Ticket Office: 0870 787-1799
Fax Number: 0870 787-3345
Web Site: www.sufc.co.uk

GENERAL INFORMATION

Car Parking: Street parking only
Coach Parking: By Police direction
Nearest Railway Station: Sheffield Midland (1 mile)
Nearest Bus Station: Pond Street, Sheffield (1 mile)
Club Shop: At the ground
Opening Times: Monday to Friday 9.00am – 5.00pm and Matchdays from 9.00am – 5.30pm
Telephone Nº: 0870 442-8705
Police Telephone Nº: (0114) 276-8522

GROUND INFORMATION

Away Supporters' Entrances & Sections:
Visitors' Box Office – Bramall Lane Stand Lower Tier

ADMISSION INFO (2006/2007 PRICES)

Adult Seating: £15.00 – £34.00
Child Seating: £10.00 – £12.00
Concessionary Seating: £10.00 – £24.00
Note: Prices vary according to the category of the game
Programme Price: £3.00

DISABLED INFORMATION

Wheelchairs: Limited number of spaces available in the disabled section – Members area
Helpers: One helper admitted per wheelchair
Prices: £10.00 for the disabled
Disabled Toilets: 3 available within the enclosure
Commentaries available for the blind on request
Contact: 0870 787-1799   (Bookings are necessary)

Travelling Supporters' Information:
Routes: From the North: Exit the M1 at Junction 33 following signs to Sheffield (A57) and continue along Sheffield Parkway until the Park Square roundabout. Take the 3rd exit and follow the A61 (Sheffield). Midland Station is on the left, the road veers to the left then take the middle lane following the ring road to the right. Take the first exit at the roundabout into Bramhall Lane.; From the South: Exit the M1 at junction 29 and take the A617 (Chesterfield). Take the 3rd exit at the roundabout onto the A61 and continue to the Earl of Arundel and Surrey Public House. Turn left and continue into Bramhall Lane; From the East: Exit the M1 at Junctions 31 or 33 and take the A57 to the roundabout, take the 3rd exit into Sheaf Street (then as from the North); From the West: Take the A57 into Sheffield and take the 4th exit at the roundabout into Upper Hanover Street and at the 2nd roundabout take the 3rd exit into Bramall Lane.

SHEFFIELD WEDNESDAY FC

Founded: 1867 (**Entered League:** 1892)
Former Name: The Wednesday FC
Nickname: 'Owls'
Ground: Hillsborough, Sheffield   S6 1SW
Ground Capacity: 39,812 (All seats)
Record Attendance: 72,841 (17/2/34)
Pitch Size: 112 × 74 yards

Colours: Blue and White striped shirts, Black shorts
Telephone Nº: 0870 999-1867
Ticket Office: 0871 230-1867
Fax Number: (0114) 221-2122
Web Site: www.swfc.co.uk
Club Call Nº: (09068) 121186

GENERAL INFORMATION

Car Parking: Street parking
Coach Parking: Clay Wheels Lane
Nearest Railway Station: Sheffield Midland (4 miles)
Nearest Bus Station: Pond Street, Sheffield (4 miles)
Club Shop: At the ground
Ground Opening Times: Monday to Friday from 8.45am to 5.15pm and Saturday from 9.00am to 12.00pm
Telephone Nº: 0870 999-1867
Telephone Nº: (0870) 999-1867
Police Telephone Nº: (0114) 220-2020

GROUND INFORMATION

Away Supporters' Entrances & Sections:
West Stand turnstiles for West Stand, Upper Tier

ADMISSION INFO (2007/2008 PRICES)

Adult Seating: £21.00 – £27.00
Child Seating: £11.00 – £16.00
Note: Discounts are available for advance bookings
Programme Price: £2.50

DISABLED INFORMATION

Wheelchairs: 257 spaces for disabled fans including 88 wheelchair spaces for home fans, and 9 wheelchair spaces for visiting fans in the disabled section – North Stand & West Stand Lower
Helpers: One helper admitted per disabled person
Prices: No charge for the disabled or helpers
Disabled Toilets: Available in the North and West Stands
Commentaries are available for the blind
Contact: (0870) 999-1867   (Bookings are necessary)

Travelling Supporters' Information:
Routes: From the North, South and East: Exit the M1 at Junction 36 and follow signs to Sheffield (A61). Continue for 4 miles then take the 3rd exit at the 2nd roundabout into Leppings Lane. The ground is situated on the left; From the West: Take the A57 until the road splits in two. Take the left fork (A6101). After 3¾ miles turn left onto the one-way system and follow the road round to the right onto Holme Lane. This road becomes Bradfield Road. At the junction with the A61 (Penistone Road), turn left towards Barnsley. The stadium is on the left after Hillsborough Park.

SHREWSBURY TOWN FC

Founded: 1886 (**Entered League**: 1950)
Nickname: 'Town'
Ground: The New Meadow, Oteley Road, Shrewsbury SY2 6ST
Ground Capacity: 10,000 (All seats)
Record Attendance: 18,917 (26th April 1961 at Gay Meadow)

Pitch Size: 116 × 75 yards
Colours: Shirts and shorts are Blue with Amber and White trim
Telephone Nº: (01743) 360111
Ticket Office: (01743) 360111
Fax Number: (01743) 236384
Web Site: www.shrewsburytown.com

GENERAL INFORMATION

Car Parking: Limited parking at the stadium – Permit Holders only. Parking restrictions are imposted on matchdays with no parking allowed in the vicinity of the stadium. Visiting fans should use the Park & Ride Scheme – cost £2.00 per person for the return journey – see below
Coach Parking: At the stadium
Nearest Railway Station: Shrewsbury (2½ miles)
Nearest Bus Station: Raven Meadows, Shrewsbury
Club Shop: At the ground
Opening Times: Matchdays and Office Hours
Telephone Nº: (01743) 360111
Police Telephone Nº: (01743) 232888

GROUND INFORMATION

Away Supporters' Entrances & Sections: North Stand

ADMISSION INFO (2007/2008 PRICES)

Adult Seating: £16.00 – £19.00
Child Seating: £11.00 – £13.00 (Cheaper for members)
Senior Citizen/Student Seating: £11.00 – £13.00
Note: Tickets are £1.00 cheaper if bought prior to the match day. A range of discounted Family Tickets are available – please contact the club for further details.
Programme Price: £2.50

DISABLED INFORMATION

Wheelchairs: Spaces in the North, South and East Stands
Helpers: One helper admitted per disabled person
Prices: £11.00 – £13.00 for the disabled. Helpers are admitted free of charge
Disabled Toilets: Available throughout the ground
Contact: (01743) 360111 (Bookings are necessary)

Travelling Supporters' Information:
Park & Ride information: Buses run every 15 minutes from 12.30pm to 2.30pm on Saturday matchdays and 6.15pm to 7.30pm on matchdays in the week. Parking is free and the return bus journey is £2.00 per person. Buses return to the car parks immediately after the match finishes and car parks will remain open for one hour only. Car Park Locations:
Oxon Park and Ride Site: From the West and North West. At the junction of the A5 and the A458 (Churncote Roundabout) follow the signs A458 'Shrewsbury Town Centre'. Oxon Park and Ride Site is clearly signposted; **The Shirehall**: From all routes proceed along the A5 to Emstrey Island Roundabout into Shrewsbury, take the A5064 along London Road to the Column roundabout. Take the 3rd exit at the roundabout and the first right into the Shirehall Car Park; **Shirehall Overflow Car Park**: Follow directions to London Road as above. Before you reach the roundabout the car park is on the right-hand side. Proceed on foot to the Shirehall main car park for the bus.

SOUTHAMPTON FC

Founded: 1885 (**Entered League:** 1920)
Former Names: Southampton St. Mary's YMCA FC (1885-1897)
Nickname: 'Saints'
Ground: St. Mary's Stadium, Britannia Road, Southampton SO14 5FP
Ground Capacity: 32,689 (All seats)
Record Attendance: 32,151 (29/12/2003)

Pitch Size: 112 × 72 yards
Colours: Red and White shirts with Black shorts
Telephone Nº: 0845 688-9448
Ticket Office: 0800 280-0050
Ticket Office Fax Number: 0845 688-9291
General Fax Number: (023) 8072-7727
Ticket Information Nº: 0845 688-9288
Web Site: www.saintsfc.co.uk

GENERAL INFORMATION

Car Parking: Park & Ride only – must be pre-booked
Coach Parking: By Police direction
Nearest Railway Station: Southampton Central
Nearest Bus Station: Western Esplanade
Club Shop: At the ground and also at West Quay
Opening Times: Monday to Saturday 9.00am – 5.00pm
Telephone Nº: 0845 688-9433
Police Telephone Nº: (023) 8033-5444

GROUND INFORMATION

Away Supporters' Entrances & Sections:
Northam Stand

ADMISSION INFO (2007/2008 PRICES)

Adult Seating: £22.00 – £28.00
Under-16s Seating: £9.00 – £28.00
Student/Senior Citizen Seating: £16.00 – £28.00
Note: Prices vary depending on the category of the game
Programme Price: £3.00

DISABLED INFORMATION

Wheelchairs: 200 spaces in total for Home and Away fans throughout the ground
Helpers: One helper admitted per disabled person
Prices: £11.00 for each disabled fan.
Disabled Toilets: Available in all Stands
Contact: (023) 8072-7777 (Bookings are necessary)
E-mail Contact: disability@saintsfc.co.uk

Travelling Supporters' Information:
Routes: Although the ground is situated in the Melbourne Street/Marine Parade area of Southampton, no parking is available in the immediate vicinity except by special arrangement for Disabled supporters. There are a number of well-signposted Park and Ride car parks around the City and those designated for Away fans should be clearly marked.

SOUTHEND UNITED FC

Founded: 1906 (**Entered League:** 1920)
Former Name: Southend Athletic FC
Nickname: 'Shrimpers' 'Blues'
Ground: Roots Hall Ground, Victoria Avenue,
Southend-on-Sea   SS2 6NQ
Ground Capacity: 12,268 (All seats)
Record Attendance: 31,033 (10/1/79)

Pitch Size: 110 × 74 yards
Colours: Shirts and shorts are Blue
Telephone Nº: (01702) 304050
Ticket Office: 08444 770077
Fax Number: (01702) 304124
Web Site: www.southendunited.co.uk

GENERAL INFORMATION

Car Parking: Car park at the ground for 500 cars – Season Ticket holders only. Otherwise use street parking
Coach Parking: Car park at the ground. Coach drivers should contact the club prior to the game
Nearest Railway Station: Prittlewell (¼ mile)
Nearest Bus Station: London Road, Southend
Club Shop: At the ground
Opening Times: Monday to Friday and Matchdays during office hours. Non-Match Saturdays 9.30am to 3.00pm
Telephone Nº: (01702) 351117
Police Telephone Nº: (01702) 431212

GROUND INFORMATION

Away Supporters' Entrances & Sections:
North Stand turnstiles for North Stand seating

ADMISSION INFO (2007/2008 PRICES)

Adult Seating: £22.00
Child Seating: £11.00
Concessionary Seating: £15.00
Note: Discounts are available for tickets bought in advance
Programme Price: £3.00

DISABLED INFORMATION

Wheelchairs: 20 spaces in total for Home and Away fans in the disabled section, West Stand
Helpers: One helper admitted per disabled person
Prices: Concessionary prices apply to disabled. Helpers receive complimentary tickets
Disabled Toilets: One available in the disabled area
Commentaries are available for the blind
Contact: 08444 770077   (Bookings are necessary)

Travelling Supporters' Information:
Routes: From the North and West: From the M25 take Junction 29 and follow the A127 to Southend. About 1 mile outside of Southend Town Centre, take the 3rd exit at the roundabout into Victoria Avenue for the ground; From the A13: Follow signs for Southend, turn left into West Road at Westcliff. At the end of West Road turn left into Victoria Avenue – the ground is on the left.

STOCKPORT COUNTY FC

Founded: 1883 (**Entered League:** 1900)
Former Names: Heaton Norris Rovers FC and Heaton Norris FC
Nickname: 'Hatters' 'County'
Ground: Edgeley Park, Hardcastle Road, Edgeley, Stockport SK3 9DD
Ground Capacity: 10,641 (All seats)
Record Attendance: 27,833 (11/2/50)

Pitch Size: 111 × 72 yards
Colours: Shirts are Blue with a White chest band, shorts are Blue with White trim
Telephone No: (0161) 286-8888
Ticket Office: (0871) 222-0120
Fax Number: (0161) 286-8900
Web Site: www.stockportcounty.com

GENERAL INFORMATION

Car Parking: Street parking
Coach Parking: By Police direction
Nearest Railway Station: Stockport (5 minutes walk)
Nearest Bus Station: Mersey Square (10 minutes walk)
Club Shop: At the ground
Opening Times: Weekdays 1.00pm – 5.30pm and Saturdays 9.30am – 1.00pm
Telephone No: (0161) 286-8899
Police Telephone No: (0161) 872-5050

GROUND INFORMATION

Away Supporters' Entrances & Sections:
Railway End turnstiles for Railway End or turnstiles for Popular Side depending on the opponents

ADMISSION INFO (2007/2008 PRICES)

Adult Seating: £16.00 – £18.00
Child Seating: £5.00
Senior Citizen Seating: £11.00
Away Fans: £16.00/£18.00 adults (depending on the game) £5.00 children, £11.00 OAPs
Programme Price: £2.50

DISABLED INFORMATION

Wheelchairs: 16 spaces in total. 10 in the Hardcastle Road Stand, 6 in the Cheadle Stand
Helpers: One helper admitted per disabled fan
Prices: £11.00 for the disabled
Disabled Toilets: Yes
Contact: (0161) 286-8888 (Bookings are necessary)

Travelling Supporters' Information:
Routes: From the North, South and West: Exit the M63 at Junction 11 and join the A560, following signs for Cheadle. After ¼ mile turn right into Edgeley Road and after 1 mile turn right into Caroline Street for the ground; From the East: Take the A6 or A560 into Stockport Town Centre and turn left into Greek Street. Take the 2nd exit into Mercian Way (from the roundabout) then turn left into Caroline Street – the ground is straight ahead.

STOKE CITY FC

Founded: 1863 (**Entered League:** 1888)
Former Name: Stoke FC
Nickname: 'Potters'
Ground: Britannia Stadium, Stanley Matthews Way, Stoke-on-Trent ST4 4EG
Ground Capacity: 28,334
Record Attendance: 28,218 (5/1/2002)

Pitch Size: 115 × 72 yards
Colours: Red and White striped shirts, White shorts
Telephone Nº: 0871 663-2008
Ticket Office: 0871 663-2007
Fax Number: (01782) 592210
Web Site: www.stokecityfc.com

GENERAL INFORMATION

Car Parking: At the ground (bookings necessary). Also various car parks within 10 minutes walk
Coach Parking: At the ground
Nearest Railway Station: Stoke-on-Trent (1½ miles)
Nearest Bus Station: Glebe Street, Stoke-on-Trent
Club Shop: At the ground
Opening Times: Monday to Friday 9.00am – 5.30pm and non-match Saturdays 9.00am–5.00pm. Saturday Matchdays 9.00am to kick-off and Final whistle to 5.30pm. Evening matchdays 9.00am to kick-off and Final whistle to 10.00pm
Telephone Nº: 0871 663-2008
Police Telephone Nº: 08453 302010

GROUND INFORMATION

Away Supporters' Sections: South Stand

ADMISSION INFO (2007/2008 PRICES)

Adult Seating: £20.00 – £27.00
Child Seating: £9.00 – £12.00 (cheaper in the Family Area)
Senior Citizen Seating: £15.00
Note: Discounted prices are available for advance bookings
Programme Price: £3.00

DISABLED INFORMATION

Wheelchairs: 112 spaces available in total
Helpers: One helper admitted per disabled person
Prices: Please contact the club for details
Disabled Toilets: Available
Commentaries are available – phone for details
Contact: 0871 663-2008   (Bookings are necessary)

Travelling Supporters' Information:
Routes: From the North, South and West: Exit the M6 at Junction 15 and take the A500 to Stoke-on-Trent. At the first exit, take the A34 to Stone and follow signs for Trentham. At the next roundabout, turn left onto Trentham Road (A5035) and carry on until you reach the junction with traffic lights which sits on the southern entrance to Stanley Matthews Way for the ground; From the East: Take the A50 to Stoke-on-Trent and leave at the Longton Exit into Trentham Road (A5035). Stay on Trentham Road until you reach the junction with traffic lights which sits on the southern entrance to Stanley Matthews Way.

SUNDERLAND AFC

Founded: 1879 (**Entered League:** 1890)
Former Names: Sunderland and District Teachers FC
Nickname: 'The Black Cats'
Ground: Stadium of Light, Sunderland   SR5 1SU
Ground Capacity: 49,000 (All seats)
Record Attendance: 48,355 (13th April 2002)
Pitch Size: 115 × 75 yards

Colours: Red and White striped shirts, Black shorts
Telephone Nº: (0191) 551-5000
Ticket Office: 0845 671-1973
Fax Number: (0191) 551-5123
Web Site: www.safc.com

GENERAL INFORMATION

Car Parking: Spaces for 1,100 cars (reserved)
Coach Parking: At the ground
Nearest Railway Station: Sunderland (1 mile)
Nearest Bus Station: Town Centre (1 mile)
Club Shop: At the Stadium, plus smaller stores in Sainsburys in Washington and Debenhams in Sunderland
Opening Times: Monday to Saturday 9.00am – 5.00pm
Telephone Nº: (0191) 551-5050
Police Telephone Nº: (0191) 510-2020

GROUND INFORMATION

Away Supporters' Entrances & Sections:
South Stand

ADMISSION INFO (2006/2007 PRICES)

Adult Seating: £17.00 to £25.00 (£30.00 for Category A)
Child Seating: £18.00 or £23.00
Note: Prices vary depending on the category of the game
Programme Price: £3.00

DISABLED INFORMATION

Wheelchairs: 180 spaces in total throughout the stadium
Helpers: Admitted
Prices: Normal prices for the disabled. Free for helpers
Disabled Toilets: Available in all stands and Corporate areas
Contact: 0845 671-1973 (Bookings are necessary)

Travelling Supporters' Information:
Routes: From All Parts: Exit the A1 at the A690 Durham/Sunderland exit. After approximately 4 miles turn left onto the A19 (signposted Tyne Tunnel). Keep in the left lane and take the slip road (signposted Washington/Sunderland) onto the bridge over the River Wear. Turn right onto the A1231 (signposted Washington/Sunderland), stay on this road going straight across 4 roundabouts into Sunderland. Continue straight through 2 sets of traffic lights and the Stadium car park is on the right, about 1 mile past the traffic lights.

SWANSEA CITY FC

Founded: 1900 (**Entered League:** 1920)
Former Name: Swansea Town FC (1900-1970)
Nickname: 'Swans'
Ground: Liberty Stadium, Landore, Swansea, SA1 2FA
Ground Capacity: 20,520 (All seats)
Record Attendance: 32,796 (at the Vetch Field)

Pitch Size: 115 × 74 yards
Colours: White shirts and shorts with Black trim
Telephone Nº: (01792) 616600
Ticket Office: (08700) 400004
Fax Number: (01792) 616606
Web Site: www.swanseacity.net

GENERAL INFORMATION

Car Parking: Reserved parking only at the stadium but 3,000 spaces are available in a Park & Ride scheme just off Junction 45 of the M4.
Coach Parking: By Police direction
Nearest Railway Station: Swansea High Street (4 miles)
Nearest Bus Station: Quadrant Depot (3 miles)
Club Shop: At the ground
Opening Times: Weekdays 10.00am – 5.30pm and Matchdays 9.30am – 5.00pm
Telephone Nº: (01792) 616616
Police Telephone Nº: (01792) 456999

GROUND INFORMATION

Away Supporters' Entrances & Sections:
North Stand

ADMISSION INFO (2007/2008 PRICES)

Adult Seating: £16.00 – £19.00
Child Seating: £7.00 – £10.00
Senior Citizen Seating: £10.00 – £13.00
Note: Special prices are available in the Family Stand and ticket prices vary depending on the category of the game
Programme Price: £3.00

DISABLED INFORMATION

Wheelchairs: 250 spaces available in total for Home and Away fans together with 250 spaces for helpers
Helpers: One helper admitted per wheelchair
Prices: Normal prices apply for the disabled. Free for helpers
Disabled Toilets: Available
There are 62 disabled parking spaces available at the stadium
Contact: (01792) 616600 (Bookings are necessary)

Travelling Supporters' Information:
Routes: From All Parts: Exit the M4 at Junction 45 and follow signs for Swansea (A4067). The stadium is clearly signposted.

SWINDON TOWN FC

Founded: 1881 (**Entered League:** 1920)
Nickname: 'Robins'
Ground: County Ground, County Road, Swindon, SN1 2ED
Ground Capacity: 14,983 (All seats)
Record Attendance: 32,000 (15th January 1972)
Pitch Size: 114 × 74 yards

Colours: Red shirts with White shorts
Telephone Nº: (0870) 443-1969
Ticket Office: (0870) 443-1894
Fax Number: (01793) 333703
Web Site: www.swindontownfc.co.uk

GENERAL INFORMATION
Car Parking: Town Centre
Coach Parking: Car park adjacent to the ground
Nearest Railway Station: Swindon (½ mile)
Nearest Bus Station: Swindon (½ mile)
Club Shop: The Swindon Town Superstore
Opening Times: Weekdays 9.00am – 5.00pm and Saturdays 10.00am – 4.00pm. Matchdays 9.00am to 3.00pm
Telephone Nº: (0870) 443-1969
Police Telephone Nº: 0845 408-7000

GROUND INFORMATION
Away Supporters' Entrances & Sections:
Arkell's Stand turnstiles for the Stratton Bank

ADMISSION INFO (2006/2007 PRICES)
Adult Seating: £15.00 – £20.00
Child Seating: £4.00 – £9.00
Concessions Seating: £12.00 – £15.00
Programme Price: £2.50

DISABLED INFORMATION
Wheelchairs: 56 spaces in total for Home and Away fans in disabled section, in front of Arkell's Stand
Helpers: One helper admitted per disabled person
Prices: Please contact the club for details
Disabled Toilets: Available within the disabled area
Commentaries are available for the blind
Contact: (0870) 443-1894 (Bookings are necessary)

Travelling Supporters' Information:
Routes: From London, the East and the South: Exit the M4 at Junction 15 and take the A345 into Swindon along Queen's Drive. Take the 3rd exit at 'Magic Roundabout' into County Road; From the West: Exit the M4 at Junction 15 then as above; From the North: Take the M4 or A345/A420/A361 to the County Road roundabout, then as above.

TOTTENHAM HOTSPUR FC

Founded: 1882 (**Entered League**: 1908)
Former Name: Hotspur FC (1882-1884)
Nickname: 'Spurs'
Ground: White Hart Lane, Bill Nicholson Way,
748 High Road, Tottenham, London N17 0AP
Ground Capacity: 36,240 (All seats)
Record Attendance: 75,038 (5/3/38)

Pitch Size: 110 × 73 yards
Colours: White shirts with Navy Blue shorts
Telephone No: (0870) 420-5000
Ticket Office: (0870) 420-5000
Fax Number: (020) 8365-5175
Web Site: www.tottenhamhotspur.com

GENERAL INFORMATION

Car Parking: None within ¼ mile of the ground
Coach Parking: Northumberland Park, Leeside Road
Nearest Railway Station: White Hart Lane (nearby) or
Northumberland Park
Nearest Tube Station: Seven Sisters (Victoria Line) or
Manor House (Piccadilly Line)
Club Shop: At the ground and also at the Essex Spurs Store,
Harvey Centre, Harlow
Opening Times: Monday to Saturday 9.30am – 5.30pm
(open from 10.00am on Monday and Tuesday). Also Sundays
10.00am – 4.00pm
Telephone No: (0870) 420-5000
Police Telephone No: (020) 8801-3443

GROUND INFORMATION

Away Supporters' Entrances & Sections:
Park Lane entrances for South Stand

ADMISSION INFO (2007/2008 PRICES)

Adult Seating: £27.00 – £71.00
Child Seating: £14.00 – £21.00 (Members only)
Senior Citizen Seating: £14.00 – £21.00
Note: Additional discounts are available for members and
prices vary depending on the category of the game
Programme Price: £3.00

DISABLED INFORMATION

Wheelchairs: 69 spaces for home fans, 8 for away fans in
the disabled areas. Home supporters' area: North Stand
West Lower Tier and South Lower; Away Supporters' area:
South Stand Lower Tier.
Helpers: One helper admitted per disabled person
Prices: £27.00 – £39.00 for one disabled person and a helper
Disabled Toilets: 4 available in the North Stand and 2
available in the South Stand
Contact: (020) 8365-5161 (Bookings are necessary)

Travelling Supporters' Information:
Routes: From All Parts: Take the A406 North Circular to Edmonton and at traffic lights follow signs for Tottenham (A1010) into
Fore Street for the ground.

TRANMERE ROVERS FC

Founded: 1885 **(Entered League:** 1921)
Former Name: Belmont FC
Nickname: 'Rovers'
Ground: Prenton Park, Prenton Road West, Birkenhead CH42 9PY
Ground Capacity: 16,789 (All seats)
Record Attendance: 24,424 (5/2/72)

Pitch Size: 110 × 70 yards
Colours: White shirts and shorts
Telephone Nº: 0870 460-3333
Ticket Office: 0870 460-3332
Fax Number: (0151) 608-4724
Web Site: www.tranmererovers.co.uk

GENERAL INFORMATION

Car Parking: Large car park at the ground (£4.00 per car)
Coach Parking: At the ground (£10.00 charge)
Nearest Railway Stations: Hamilton Square, Rock Ferry and Conway Park (approximately 1½ miles)
Nearest Bus Station: Conway Park (Town Centre)
Club Shop: At the ground
Opening Times: Weekdays 9.30am–5.00pm, Matchdays 10.00am–kick-off, non-Saturday matchdays 10.00am–1.00pm
Telephone Nº: 0870 460-3331
Police Telephone Nº: (0151) 709-6010

GROUND INFORMATION

Away Supporters' Entrances & Sections:
Cowshed Stand turnstiles 5-9 – access from Borough Road (Away section capacity: 2,500)

ADMISSION INFO (2007/2008 PRICES)

Adult Seating: £12.00 – £21.00
Child Seating: £5.00
Concessionary Seating (Seniors 60+): £8.00 – £10.00
Young Persons Ticket (Ages 17-22): £8.00 – £14.00
Programme Price: £2.50
Note: Senior Citizen or Young Person tickets must be purchased from the Ticket Office prior to the game

DISABLED INFORMATION

Wheelchairs: 28 spaces in total for Home and Away fans in the disabled section, Paddock – Family Stand
Helpers: One helper admitted per disabled person
Prices: Adults £5.00 Concessions £2.50
Disabled Toilets: 2 available in the disabled section
Contact: 0870 460-3332 (Bookings are necessary)

Travelling Supporters' Information:
Routes: From the North: Take the Mersey Tunnel (Queensway), bear right onto the flyover after the tollbooths and continue on to Borough Road. Continue on Borough Road for approximately 1 mile and the ground is situated on the right; From the South and East: Exit the M53 at Junction 4 and take the 3rd exit at roundabout (B5151). After 2½ miles turn right into Prenton Road West for the ground.

WALSALL FC

Founded: 1888 (**Entered League:** 1892)
Former Name: Walsall Town Swifts FC (1888-1895)
Nickname: 'Saddlers'
Ground: Banks's Stadium, Bescot Crescent, Walsall, West Midlands WS1 4SA
Ground Capacity: 11,300 (All seats)
Record Attendance: 11,037 (11th January 2003)
Pitch Size: 110 × 73 yards

Colours: White shirts with Red shorts
Telephone Nº: 0871 221-0442
Ticket Office: 0871 663-0111 or 0871 663-0222
Fax Number: (01922) 613202
Web Site: www.saddlers.co.uk
Club Call Nº: (09068) 555800

GENERAL INFORMATION

Car Parking: Car park at the ground
Coach Parking: At the ground
Nearest Railway Station: Bescot (adjacent)
Nearest Bus Station: Bradford Place, Walsall
Club Shop: At the ground and in Bradford Street, Walsall
Opening Times: Weekdays and Matchdays 9.00am–5.00pm
Telephone Nº: (01922) 631072 (Bradford Street)
Police Telephone Nº: (01922) 638111

GROUND INFORMATION

Away Supporters' Entrances & Sections:
Turnstiles 21-28 for Homeserve Stand accommodation

ADMISSION INFO (2007/2008 PRICES)

Adult Seating: £15.00 – £19.00
Child Seating: £11.00 – £13.00
Concessionary Seating: £11.00 – £14.00
Note: Discounts are available for advance bookings and savings from Family Tickets are available in some stands
Programme Price: £2.50

DISABLED INFORMATION

Wheelchairs: 30 spaces in total for Home and Away fans in the disabled section, West Bromwich Building Society Stand
Helpers: One helper admitted per disabled person
Prices: £19.00 for wheelchair disabled (discounts available for advance bookings). Free of charge for helpers
Disabled Toilets: Adjacent to disabled viewing bays
A special Lounge for fans with disabilities is available
Contact: 0871 663-0222 (Bookings are necessary)

Travelling Supporters' Information:
Routes: From All Parts: Exit the M6 at Junction 9 turning North towards Walsall onto the A461. After ¼ mile turn right into Wallows Lane and pass over the railway bridge. Then take the 1st right into Bescot Crescent and the ground is ½ mile along on the left adjacent to Bescot Railway Station.

WATFORD FC

Founded: 1881 (**Entered League:** 1920)
Former Names: Formed by the amalgamation of West Herts FC and St. Mary's FC
Nickname: 'Hornets'
Ground: Vicarage Road Stadium, Watford, WD18 0ER
Ground Capacity: 19,920 (All seats)
Record Attendance: 34,099 (3/2/69)

Pitch Size: 115 × 75 yards
Colours: Yellow shirts with Black shorts
Telephone No: 0845 442-1881
Ticket Office: 0845 442-1881
Fax Number: (01923) 496001
Web Site: www.watfordfc.com

GENERAL INFORMATION

Car Parking: Nearby multi-storey car parks and schools
Coach Parking: By Police direction
Nearest Railway Station: Watford Junction or Watford Tube Station (Metropolitan Line)
Nearest Bus Station: Watford Town Centre
Club Shop: At the ground
Opening Times: Weekdays and Matchdays 9.00am–5.30pm
Telephone No: 0870 111-1881
Police Telephone No: (01923) 472000

GROUND INFORMATION

Away Supporters' Entrances & Sections:
Vicarage Road End entrances and accommodation

ADMISSION INFO (2007/2008 PRICES)

Adult Seating: £10.00 – £25.00
Child Seating: £1.00 – £10.00
Senior Citizen Seating: £10.00 – £15.00
Programme Price: £3.00

DISABLED INFORMATION

Wheelchairs: 40 spaces in total in the disabled sections, South East Corner and North Stand
Helpers: One helper admitted per disabled person
Prices: £10.00 – £20.00 for the disabled. Free for helpers
Disabled Toilets: Adjacent to disabled enclosures
Commentaries available in East Stand – no charge
Contact: 0845 442-1881 (Bookings in advance helpful)

Travelling Supporters' Information:
Routes: From the North: Exit the M1 at Junction 5 and take the new road (A4008) towards Watford Town Centre. This will take you around the ring road, follow signs for Watford General Hospital. The ground is next to the hospital; From the South: Exit M1 at Junction 5 (then as North); From the East: Exit the M25 at Junction 21A and join the M1 at Junction 6. Exit at Junction 5 (then as North); From the West: Exit the M25 at Junction 19 and take the third exit off the roundabout onto the A411 (Hempstead Road) signposted for Watford. Continue for approximately two miles and go straight on at the roundabout (enter the right-hand lane) for the next roundabout and take the third exit into Rickmansworth Road. Take the second turning on the left into Cassio Road. Go through the traffic lights into Merton Road and follow signs for Watford General Hospital into Vicarage Road.

WEST BROMWICH ALBION FC

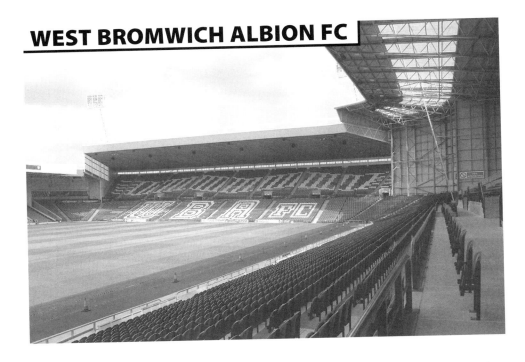

Founded: 1879 (**Entered League:** 1888)
Former Name: West Bromwich Strollers (1879-1880)
Nickname: 'Throstles' 'Baggies' 'Albion'
Ground: The Hawthorns, Halfords Lane,
West Bromwich, West Midlands   B71 4LF
Ground Capacity: 28,000 (All seats)
Record Attendance: 64,815 (6/3/37)

Pitch Size: 115 × 74 yards
Colours: Navy Blue & White striped shirts, White shorts
Telephone Nº: 0871 271-1100
Ticket Office: 0871 271-9780
Fax Number: 0871 271-9848
Web Site: www.wba.co.uk

GENERAL INFORMATION

Car Parking: Halfords Lane Car Parks, East Stand Car Park
and several independent car parks
Coach Parking: At the ground
Nearest Railway Station: Hawthorns (200 yards) or
Rolfe Street, Smethwick (1½ miles)
Nearest Midland Metro: Hawthorns (200 yards)
Nearest Bus Station: West Bromwich Town Centre
Club Shop: At the ground and at the Merry Hill Centre
Opening Times: Weekdays 9.00am – 5.00pm and Saturday
Matchdays 9.00am – 2.45pm
Telephone Nº: 0871 271-9790
Police Telephone Nº: (0121) 554-3414

GROUND INFORMATION

Away Supporters' Entrances & Sections:
Smethwick End 'A' turnstiles

ADMISSION INFO (2007/2008 PRICES)

Adult Seating: £23.00 – £28.00
Child Seating: £11.00 – £14.00
Senior Citizen Seating: £14.00 – £17.00
Student Seating: £14.00 – £17.00
Programme Price: £3.00

DISABLED INFORMATION

Wheelchairs: 150 spaces in total in the disabled sections,
Birmingham Road End, Smethwick End and the East Stand
Helpers: One helper admitted per disabled person (subject
to availability of space)
Prices: £11.00 – £13.00 for the disabled. Free for helpers
Disabled Toilets: Available within disabled section
Commentaries are available in the Halfords Lane Stand
Contact: 08700 668888   (Bookings are necessary)

Travelling Supporters' Information:
Routes: From All Parts: Exit the M5 at Junction 1 and follow Matchday signs for the ground. The matchday traffic plan has
made the "obvious" route via the A41 unusable for home games.

WEST HAM UNITED FC

Founded: 1895 (**Entered League**: 1919)
Former Name: Thames Iron Works FC
Nickname: 'Hammers'
Ground: Boleyn Ground, Green Street, Upton Park, London   E13 9AZ
Ground Capacity: 35,303 (All seats)
Record Attendance: 42,322 (17/10/70)

Pitch Size: 110 × 70 yards
Colours: Claret and Blue shirts with White shorts
Telephone Nº: (020) 8548-2748
Ticket Office: (0870) 112-2700
Fax Number: (020) 8548-2758
Web Site: www.whufc.com

GENERAL INFORMATION

Car Parking: Street parking
Coach Parking: By Police direction
Nearest Railway Station: Barking
Nearest Tube Station: Upton Park (5 minutes walk)
Club Shops: At the Stadium and also at Lakeside
Opening Times: Weekdays and Matchdays 9.30am–5.00pm
Telephone Nº: (020) 8548-2794 (Stadium Store);
(01708) 890258 (Lakeside Store)
Mail-Order Nº: (0870) 112-2700
Police Telephone Nº: (020) 8593-8232

GROUND INFORMATION

Away Supporters' Entrances & Sections:
Priory Road entrance for the Centenary Stand

ADMISSION INFO (2007/2008 PRICES)

Adult Seating: £34.00 – £61.00
Child Seating: £17.00 – £30.50
Senior Citizen Seating: £20.00 – £33.50
Note: Prices vary depending on the category of the game
Programme Price: £3.00

DISABLED INFORMATION

Wheelchairs: 150 spaces for home fans, 12 spaces for away fans in the disabled area, Centenary Stand
Helpers: Admitted
Prices: £17.00 for the disabled. Free of charge for helpers
Disabled Toilets: 12 available
Contact: Gina Allen (020) 8548-2725 (Bookings necessary)

Travelling Supporters' Information:
Routes: From the North and West: Take the North Circular (A406) to the A124 (East Ham) then along Barking Road for approximately 1½ miles until approaching the traffic lights at the crossroad. Turn right into Green Street, the ground is on the right-hand side; From the South: Take the Blackwall Tunnel and the A13 to Canning Town. Follow signs for East Ham (A124). After 1¾ miles turn left into Green Street; From the East: Take the A13 and turn right onto the A117 at the crossroads. After approximately 1 mile turn left at the crossroads onto the A124. Turn right after ¾ mile into Green Street for the ground.

WIGAN ATHLETIC FC

Founded: 1932 (**Entered League**: 1978)
Nickname: 'Latics'
Ground: JJB Stadium, Robin Park, Newtown, Wigan, Lancashire   WN5 0UZ
Ground Capacity: 25,138 (All seats)
Record Attendance: 25,023 (11th February 2006)
Pitch Size: 115 × 74 yards

Colours: Blue and White striped shirts, Blue shorts
Telephone Nº: (01942) 774000
Ticket Office: 0871 663-3552
Fax Number: (01942) 770477
Web Site: www.wiganathletic.tv

GENERAL INFORMATION

Car Parking: 2,500 spaces available at the ground (£5.00)
Coach Parking: At the ground
Nearest Railway Station: Wallgate and Wigan North Western (1 mile)
Nearest Bus Station: Wigan
Club Shop: At all JJB Sports Stores in Wigan
Opening Times: Weekdays 9.00am to 5.00pm and Matchdays 10.00am – 5.00pm
Police Telephone Nº: (0161) 872-5050

GROUND INFORMATION

Away Supporters' Entrances & Sections: North Stand

ADMISSION INFO (2006/2007 PRICES)

Adult Seating: £22.00 – £35.00
Child/Senior Citizen Seating: £12.00 – £30.00
JJ's Club: £5.00 – £10.00 (Children only)
Note: Prices vary depending on the category of the game
Programme Price: £3.00

DISABLED INFORMATION

Wheelchairs: 25 spaces available in each stand
Helpers: One helper admitted per disabled person
Prices: £18.00 – £30.00 for each disabled fan + a helper
Disabled Toilets: Available in every stand
Contact: (01942) 774000   (Bookings are necessary)

Travelling Supporters' Information:
Routes: From North: Exit M6 at Junction 27, turn left at end of slip road then right at T-junction, signposted Shevington. After 1 mile turn left at the mini-roundabout into Old Lane (B5375). After approx. 2 miles winding through countryside turn right at traffic lights into Scot Lane. Stadium is next left; From South & West: Exit M6 at Junction 25 follow signs for Wigan (A49). After approx. 2 miles a complex junction is reached, keep in left-hand lane (McDonalds on right). Turn left at traffic light filter lane into Robin Park Road. Turn right at third set of traffic lights and follow road to stadium; From East: Exit M61 Junction 6, take 1st exit at roundabout. At next roundabout take 1st left into Chorley Road. Follow signs for Wigan B5238, first turning right then left at Aspull Roundabout. After 2 miles turn right at traffic lights after Earl of Balcarres Pub to face Tesco. Turn left at lights, keep in left lane turn left at next lights with the Quality Hotel on the corner. Follow ring road, get into second lane from right as road bears right into Caroline Street, signposted Orrell. Continue on ring road as it bears left passing B&Q on left, pass Wigan Pier on right and as road goes under railway bridge get into right hand lane to turn right at lights into Robin Park Road. Then South & West.

WOLVERHAMPTON WANDERERS FC

Founded: 1877 (**Entered League**: 1888)
Former Names: Formed by the amalgamation of St. Luke's FC and The Wanderers Football and Cricket Club in 1879. St. Luke's is considered the start of the club
Nickname: 'Wolves'
Ground: Molineux Stadium, Waterloo Road, Wolverhampton WV1 4QR
Ground Capacity: 28,576 (All seats)

Record Attendance: 61,315 (11/2/39)
Pitch Size: 110 × 75 yards
Colours: Gold shirts with Black shorts
Telephone Nº: 0871 880-8442
Ticket Office: 0871 880-8433
Fax Number: (01902) 687006
Web Site: www.wolves.co.uk

GENERAL INFORMATION

Car Parking: Around West Park, Newhampton Road and rear of the Stan Cullis Stand. Also in City Centre (5 minutes walk)
Coach Parking: By Police direction
Nearest Railway Station: Wolverhampton (¾ mile)
Nearest Bus Station: Wolverhampton (¾ mile)
Club Shop: At the ground and in the City Centre
Opening Times: Daily from 9.00am – 5.00pm
Telephone Nº: 0871 880-8442
Police Telephone Nº: (01902) 649000

GROUND INFORMATION

Away Supporters' Entrances & Sections:
Jack Harris turnstiles for Block 5 or Steve Bull Stand Lower Tier (turnstiles for Block 3)

ADMISSION INFO (2007/2008 PRICES)

Adult Seating: £23.00 – £29.00
Child/Senior Citizen Seating: £13.00 – £17.00
Programme Price: £3.00

DISABLED INFORMATION

Wheelchairs: 104 spaces in total in the disabled sections, Stan Cullis Stand and Billy Wright Family Enclosure
Helpers: Admitted
Prices: Please contact the club for details
Disabled Toilets: At both ends of the Stan Cullis Stand
Commentaries for the blind available from local radio
Contact: (0870) 442-0123 (Lindsey Beckett)
(Bookings are necessary)

Travelling Supporters' Information:
Routes: From North: Exit M6 Junction 12. At island take 3rd exit onto A5 for Wolverhampton. At next island turn left onto A449. After 6 miles A449 passes under M54, carry straight on and at 6th roundabout (Five Ways) take 3rd exit into Waterloo Road. Molineux is 1 mile straight on; From South West: Exit M5 Junction 2, follow signs for Wolverhampton on A4123 for 8 miles to ring road. Turn left on ring road (follow Molineux Centre signs). Take 2nd exit at next 2 islands * Pass Bank's Brewery and Swimming Baths on left and turn left at next set of traffic lights. Molineux is 500 yards on right; From South/East: Exit M6 Junction 10, take A454 (via Willenhall) to Wolverhampton ring road. At first ring road island take 4th exit (A449 to Stafford). Straight on at next 2 sets of traffic lights. Filter right at third set of lights (Waterloo Road). Molineux is 500 yards on right; From West: Take A41 to Wolverhampton ring road roundabout. Turn left into the ring road. Then as from the South West *

WREXHAM FC

Founded: 1872 (**Entered League**: 1921)
Nickname: 'Red Dragons'
Ground: Racecourse Ground, Mold Road, Wrexham, North Wales LL11 2AH
Ground Capacity: 10,500 (all seats) at present as the ground undergoes re-development
Record Attendance: 34,445 (26/1/57)

Pitch Size: 111 × 71 yards
Colours: Red shirts with White shorts
Telephone Nº: (01978) 262129
Fax Number: (01978) 357821
Web Site: www.wrexhamfc.tv

GENERAL INFORMATION

Car Parking: Town car parks are nearby and also Newi College (Mold End)
Coach Parking: By Police direction
Nearest Railway Station: Wrexham General (adjacent)
Nearest Bus Station: Wrexham (King Street)
Club Shop: At the ground, under the Main Stand
Opening Times: Office hours only
Telephone Nº: (01978) 262129
Police Telephone Nº: (01978) 290222

GROUND INFORMATION

Away Supporters' Entrances & Sections:
Turnstiles 36-42 for the Eric Roberts (Builders) Stand

ADMISSION INFO (2007/2008 PRICES)

Adult Seating: £16.00 – £17.00
Child Seating: £5.00
Senior Citizen Seating: £10.00
Programme Price: £2.50

DISABLED INFORMATION

Wheelchairs: 35 spaces in the Pryce Griffiths Stand
Helpers: One helper admitted per wheelchair
Prices: £10.00 for the disabled. Free of charge for helpers
Disabled Toilets: Available in the disabled section
Contact: (01978) 351332 (Tony Millington) (Please book)

Travelling Supporters' Information:
Routes: From the North and West: Take the A483 and the Wrexham bypass to the junction with the A541. Branch left at the roundabout and follow Wrexham signs into Mold Road; From the East: Take the A525 or A534 into Wrexham then follow the A541 signs into Mold Road; From the South: Take the the M6, then the M54 and follow the A5 and A483 to the Wrexham bypass and the junction with the A541. Branch right at the roundabout and follow signs for the Town Centre.

WYCOMBE WANDERERS FC

Founded: 1884 (**Entered League**: 1993)
Nickname: 'The Blues' 'The Chairboys'
Ground: Adams Park, Hillbottom Road, Sands, High Wycombe   HP12 4HJ
Ground Capacity: 10,000
Seating Capacity: 8,250
Record Attendance: 9,971 (10th January 2007)

Pitch Size: 115 × 75 yards
Colours: Navy and Light Blue quarters with Navy shorts
Telephone Nº: (01494) 472100
Ticket Office: (01494) 441118
Fax Number: (01494) 527633
Web Site: www.wycombewanderers.co.uk

GENERAL INFORMATION

Car Parking: Car park at the ground
Coach Parking: Car park at the ground
Nearest Railway Station: High Wycombe
Nearest Bus Station: High Wycombe
Club Shop: At the ground
Opening Times: Weekdays and Matchdays
Telephone Nº: (01494) 472100
Police Telephone Nº: (01494) 465888

ADMISSION INFO (2007/2008 PRICES)

Adult Standing: £14.00
Adult Seating: £16.00–£21.00
Child Standing: £6.00
Child Seating: £6.00 – £16.00
Concessionary Standing: £14.00
Concessionary Seating: £14.00 –£16.00
Note: A £2.00 discount is available for pre-booked tickets
Programme Price: £2.50

GROUND INFORMATION

Away Supporters' Entrances & Sections:
Dreams Stand (seating only)

DISABLED INFORMATION

Wheelchairs: 50 spaces in total available in the disabled section of the Family Stand
Helpers: One helper admitted per wheelchair
Prices: Free for the disabled. Full price for helpers
Disabled Toilets: Available in the New Family Stand
Commentaries are available for 5 people
Contact: (01494) 472100   (Bookings are necessary)

Travelling Supporters' Information:
Routes: From All Parts: Exit the M40 at Junction 4 and take the A4010 following Aylesbury signs. Go straight on at 3 mini-roundabouts then bear sharp left at the 4th roundabout into Lane End Road. Fork right into Hillbottom Road at the next roundabout. The ground is at the end of the road. Hillbottom Road is on the Sands Industrial Estate; From the Town Centre: Take the A40 West and after 1½ miles turn left into Chapel Lane (after the traffic lights). Turn right then right again at the mini-roundabout into Lane End Road – then as above.

YEOVIL TOWN FC

Founded: 1895
Former Names: Yeovil & Petters United FC
Nickname: 'Glovers'
Ground: Huish Park Stadium, Lufton Way, Yeovil, Somerset BA22 8YF
Ground Capacity: 9,665
Seating Capacity: 5,485

Record Attendance: 9,348 (4th January 2004)
Pitch Size: 115 × 72 yards
Colours: Green and White shirts with Green shorts
Telephone Nº: (01935) 423662
Ticket Office Nº: (01935) 847888
Fax Number: (01935) 473956
Web site: www.ytfc.net

GENERAL INFORMATION

Car Parking: Spaces for 1,000 cars at the ground
Coach Parking: At the ground
Nearest Railway Station: Yeovil Pen Mill (2½ miles) and Yeovil Junction (3½ miles)
Nearest Bus Station: Yeovil (2 miles)
Club Shop: At the ground
Opening Times: Weekdays 9.00am – 5.00pm and Matchdays 10.00am – 3.00pm
Telephone Nº: (01935) 423662
Police Telephone Nº: (01935) 415291

GROUND INFORMATION

Away Supporters' Entrances & Sections:
Copse Road End (turnstiles 13-16) & Main Stand (turnstile 1)

ADMISSION INFO (2007/2008 PRICES)

Adult Standing: £17.00 – £18.00
Adult Seating: £18.00 – £19.00
Child Standing: £6.00
Child Seating: £6.00 (Junior Glovers £3.00)
Senior Citizen Standing: £12.00 – £13.00
Senior Citizen Seating: £14.00 – £16.00
Note: Discounts are available for tickets purchased in advance
Programme Price: £2.50

DISABLED INFORMATION

Wheelchairs: 15 spaces for home fans, 5 spaces for away fans
Helpers: Admitted free of charge
Prices: Please phone the club for information
Disabled Toilets: Two are available
Contact: (01935) 847888 (Bookings are recommended)

Travelling Supporters' Information:
Routes: From London: Take the M3 and A303 to Cartgate Roundabout. Enter Yeovil on the A3088. Exit left at the 1st roundabout then straight over the next two roundabouts into Western Avenue. Cross the next roundabout then turn left into Copse Road, where supporters' parking is sited; From the North: Exit the M5 at Junction 25 and take the A358 (Ilminster) and A303 (Eastbound) entering Yeovil on the A3088. Then as above.

F.A. Premier League 2006/2007 Season	Arsenal	Aston Villa	Blackburn Rovers	Bolton Wanderers	Charlton Athletic	Chelsea	Everton	Fulham	Liverpool	Manchester City	Manchester United	Middlesbrough	Newcastle United	Portsmouth	Reading	Sheffield United	Tottenham Hotspur	Watford	West Ham United	Wigan Athletic
Arsenal	■	1-1	6-2	2-1	4-0	1-1	1-1	3-1	3-0	3-1	2-1	1-1	1-1	2-2	2-1	3-0	3-0	3-0	0-1	2-1
Aston Villa	0-1	■	2-0	0-1	2-0	0-0	1-1	1-1	0-0	1-3	0-3	1-1	2-0	0-0	2-1	3-0	1-1	2-0	1-0	1-1
Blackburn Rovers	0-2	1-2	■	0-1	4-1	0-2	1-1	2-0	1-0	4-2	0-1	2-1	1-3	3-0	3-3	2-1	1-1	3-1	1-2	2-1
Bolton Wanderers	3-1	2-2	1-2	■	1-1	0-1	1-1	2-1	2-0	0-0	0-4	0-0	2-1	3-2	1-3	1-0	2-0	1-0	4-0	0-1
Charlton Athletic	1-2	2-1	1-0	2-0	■	0-1	1-1	2-2	0-3	1-0	0-3	1-3	2-0	0-1	0-0	1-1	0-2	0-0	4-0	1-0
Chelsea	1-1	1-1	3-0	2-2	2-1	■	1-1	2-2	1-0	3-0	0-0	3-0	1-0	2-1	2-2	3-0	1-0	4-0	1-0	4-0
Everton	1-0	0-1	1-0	1-0	2-1	2-3	■	4-1	3-0	1-1	2-4	0-0	3-0	3-0	1-1	2-0	1-2	2-1	2-0	2-2
Fulham	2-1	1-1	1-1	1-1	2-1	0-2	1-0	■	1-0	1-3	1-2	2-1	2-1	1-1	0-1	1-0	1-1	0-0	0-0	0-1
Liverpool	4-1	3-1	1-1	3-0	2-2	2-0	0-0	4-0	■	1-0	0-1	2-0	2-0	0-0	2-0	4-0	3-0	2-0	2-1	2-0
Manchester City	1-0	0-2	0-3	0-2	0-0	0-1	2-1	3-1	0-0	■	0-1	1-0	0-0	0-2	0-0	1-2	0-0	2-0	0-1	
Manchester United	0-1	3-1	4-1	4-1	2-0	1-1	3-0	5-1	2-0	3-1	■	1-1	2-0	3-0	3-2	2-0	1-0	4-0	0-1	3-1
Middlesbrough	1-1	1-3	0-1	5-1	2-0	2-1	2-1	3-1	0-0	0-2	1-2	■	1-0	0-4	2-1	3-1	2-3	4-1	1-0	1-1
Newcastle United	0-0	3-1	0-2	1-2	0-0	0-0	1-1	1-2	2-1	0-1	2-2	0-0	■	1-0	3-2	0-1	3-1	2-1	2-2	2-1
Portsmouth	0-0	2-2	3-0	0-1	0-1	0-2	2-0	1-1	2-1	2-1	2-1	0-0	2-1	■	3-1	3-1	1-1	2-1	2-0	1-0
Reading	0-4	2-0	1-2	1-0	2-0	0-1	0-2	1-0	1-2	1-0	1-1	3-2	1-0	0-0	■	3-1	3-1	0-2	6-0	3-2
Sheffield United	1-0	2-2	0-0	2-2	2-1	0-2	1-1	2-0	1-1	0-1	1-2	2-1	1-2	1-1	1-2	■	2-1	1-0	3-0	1-2
Tottenham Hotspur	2-2	2-1	1-1	4-1	5-1	2-1	0-2	0-0	0-1	2-1	0-4	2-1	2-3	2-1	1-0	2-0	■	3-1	1-0	3-1
Watford	1-2	0-0	2-1	0-1	2-2	0-1	0-3	3-3	0-3	1-1	1-2	2-0	1-1	4-2	0-0	0-1	0-0	■	1-1	1-1
West Ham United	1-0	1-1	2-1	3-1	3-1	1-4	1-0	3-3	1-2	0-1	1-0	2-0	0-2	1-2	0-1	1-0	3-4	0-1	■	0-2
Wigan Athletic	0-1	0-0	0-3	1-3	3-2	2-3	0-2	0-0	0-4	4-0	1-3	0-1	1-0	1-0	1-0	0-1	3-3	1-1	0-3	■

Football League The Championship 2006/2007 Season	Barnsley	Birmingham City	Burnley	Cardiff City	Colchester United	Coventry City	Crystal Palace	Derby County	Hull City	Ipswich Town	Leeds United	Leicester City	Luton Town	Norwich City	Plymouth Argyle	Preston North End	Queen's Park Rangers	Sheffield Wednesday	Southampton	Southend United	Stoke City	Sunderland	West Bromwich Albion
Barnsley		1-0	1-0	1-2	0-3	0-1	2-0	1-2	3-0	1-0	3-2	0-1	1-2	1-3	2-2	0-1	2-0	0-3	2-2	2-0	2-2	0-2	1-⋯
Birmingham City	2-0		0-1	1-0	2-1	3-0	2-1	1-0	2-1	2-2	1-0	1-1	2-2	0-1	3-0	3-1	2-1	2-0	2-1	1-3	1-0	1-1	2-⋯
Burnley	4-2	1-2		2-0	1-2	1-2	1-1	0-0	2-0	1-0	2-1	0-1	0-0	3-0	4-0	3-2	2-0	1-1	2-3	0-0	0-1	2-2	3-⋯
Cardiff City	2-0	2-0	1-0		0-0	1-0	0-0	2-2	0-1	2-2	1-0	3-2	4-1	1-0	2-2	4-1	0-1	1-2	1-0	0-1	1-1	0-1	1-⋯
Colchester United	1-2	1-1	0-0	3-1		0-0	0-2	4-3	5-1	2-1	1-1	4-1	3-0	0-1	1-0	2-1	4-0	2-0	3-0	3-0	3-1	1-⋯	⋯
Coventry City	4-1	0-1	1-0	2-2	2-1		2-4	1-2	2-0	1-2	1-0	0-0	1-0	3-0	0-1	0-4	0-1	3-1	2-1	1-1	0-0	2-1	0-⋯
Crystal Palace	2-0	0-1	2-2	1-2	1-3	1-0		2-0	1-1	2-0	1-0	2-0	2-1	3-1	0-1	3-0	3-0	1-2	0-2	3-1	0-1	1-0	0-⋯
Derby County	2-1	0-1	1-0	3-1	5-1	1-1	1-0		2-2	2-1	2-0	1-0	0-0	1-0	1-1	1-1	1-0	2-2	3-0	0-2	1-2	2-⋯	⋯
Hull City	2-3	2-0	2-0	4-1	1-1	0-1	1-1	1-2		2-5	1-2	1-2	0-0	1-2	1-2	2-0	2-1	2-1	2-4	4-0	0-2	0-1	0-⋯
Ipswich Town	5-1	1-0	1-1	3-1	3-2	2-1	1-2	2-1	0-0		1-0	0-2	5-0	3-1	3-0	2-3	2-1	0-2	2-1	0-2	0-1	3-1	1-⋯
Leeds United	2-2	3-2	1-0	0-1	3-0	2-1	2-1	0-1	0-0	1-1		1-2	1-0	1-0	2-1	2-1	0-0	2-3	0-3	2-0	0-4	0-3	2-⋯
Leicester City	2-0	1-2	0-1	0-0	0-0	3-0	1-1	1-1	0-1	3-1	1-1		1-1	1-2	2-2	0-1	1-3	1-4	3-2	1-0	2-1	0-2	1-⋯
Luton Town	0-2	3-2	0-2	0-0	1-1	3-1	2-1	0-2	1-2	0-2	5-1	2-0		2-3	1-2	2-0	2-3	3-2	0-2	0-0	2-2	0-5	2-⋯
Norwich City	5-1	1-0	1-4	1-0	1-1	1-1	0-1	1-2	1-1	1-1	2-1	3-1	3-2		1-3	2-0	1-0	1-2	0-1	0-0	1-0	1-0	1-⋯
Plymouth Argyle	2-4	0-1	0-0	3-3	3-0	3-2	1-0	3-1	1-0	1-1	1-2	3-0	1-0	3-1		2-0	1-1	1-2	1-1	2-1	1-1	0-2	2-⋯
Preston North End	1-0	1-0	2-0	2-1	1-0	1-1	0-0	1-2	2-1	1-0	4-1	0-1	3-0	2-1	3-0		1-1	0-0	3-1	2-3	3-2	4-1	1-⋯
Queens Park Rangers	1-0	0-2	3-1	1-0	1-0	0-1	4-2	1-2	2-0	1-3	2-2	1-1	3-2	3-3	1-1	1-0		1-1	0-2	2-0	1-1	1-2	1-⋯
Sheffield Wednesday	2-1	0-3	1-1	0-0	2-0	2-1	3-2	1-2	1-2	2-0	0-1	2-1	0-1	3-2	1-1	1-3	3-2		3-3	3-2	1-1	2-4	3-1
Southampton	5-2	4-3	0-0	2-2	1-2	2-0	1-1	0-1	0-0	1-0	1-0	2-0	2-1	2-1	1-0	1-1	1-2	2-1		4-1	1-0	1-2	0-⋯
Southend United	1-3	0-4	1-0	0-3	0-3	2-3	0-1	0-1	2-3	1-3	1-1	2-2	1-3	3-3	1-1	0-0	5-0	0-0	2-1		1-0	3-1	3-1
Stoke City	0-1	0-0	0-1	3-0	3-1	1-0	2-1	2-0	1-1	0-0	3-1	4-2	0-0	5-0	1-1	1-0	1-2	2-1	1-1		2-1	1-0
Sunderland	2-0	0-1	3-2	1-2	3-1	2-0	0-0	2-1	2-0	1-0	2-0	1-1	2-1	1-0	2-3	0-1	2-1	1-0	1-1	4-0	2-2		2-⋯
West Bromwich Albion	7-0	1-1	3-0	1-0	2-1	5-0	2-3	1-0	2-0	2-0	4-2	2-0	3-2	0-1	2-1	4-2	3-3	0-1	1-1	1-1	1-3	1-2	
Wolverhampton Wanderers	2-0	2-3	2-1	1-2	1-0	1-0	1-1	0-1	3-1	1-0	1-0	1-2	0-2	2-2	2-2	1-3	2-0	2-2	0-6	3-1	2-0	1-1	1-0

ll League

One

007 Season

	AFC Bournemouth	Blackpool	Bradford City	Brentford	Brighton & Hove Albion	Bristol City	Carlisle United	Cheltenham Town	Chesterfield	Crewe Alexandra	Doncaster Rovers	Gillingham	Huddersfield Town	Leyton Orient	Millwall	Northampton Town	Nottingham Forest	Oldham Athletic	Port Vale	Rotherham United	Scunthorpe United	Swansea City	Tranmere Rovers	Yeovil Town
AFC Bournemouth		1-3	1-1	1-0	1-0	0-1	0-1	2-1	0-3	1-0	2-0	1-1	1-2	5-0	1-0	0-0	2-0	3-2	0-4	1-3	1-1	2-2	2-0	0-2
Blackpool	2-0		4-1	1-3	0-0	0-1	2-1	2-1	1-1	2-1	3-1	1-1	3-1	3-0	0-1	4-1	0-2	2-2	2-1	0-1	3-1	1-1	3-2	1-1
Bradford City	0-0	1-3		1-1	2-3	2-1	1-1	2-2	1-0	0-1	0-1	4-2	0-1	0-2	2-2	1-2	2-2	1-1	2-0	1-1	0-1	2-2	2-0	0-2
Brentford	0-0	1-0	2-1		1-0	1-1	0-0	0-2	2-1	0-4	0-4	2-2	2-2	2-2	1-4	0-1	2-4	2-2	4-3	0-1	0-2	0-2	1-1	1-2
Brighton & Hove Albion	2-2	0-3	0-1	2-2		0-2	1-2	2-1	1-2	1-4	0-2	1-0	0-0	4-1	0-1	1-1	2-1	1-2	0-0	0-0	1-1	3-2	0-1	1-3
Bristol City	2-2	2-4	2-3	1-0	1-0		1-0	0-1	3-1	2-1	1-0	3-1	1-1	2-1	1-0	1-0	1-1	0-0	2-1	3-1	1-0	0-0	3-2	2-0
Carlisle United	3-1	2-0	1-0	2-0	3-1	1-3		2-0	0-0	0-2	1-0	5-0	1-1	3-1	1-2	1-1	1-0	1-1	3-2	1-1	0-2	1-2	1-0	1-4
Cheltenham Town	1-0	1-2	1-2	2-0	1-1	2-2	0-1		0-0	1-1	0-2	1-1	2-1	2-1	3-2	0-2	0-2	1-2	0-1	2-0	1-1	2-1	1-0	1-2
Chesterfield	0-1	2-0	3-0	3-1	0-1	1-3	0-0	1-0		2-1	1-1	0-1	0-0	0-1	5-1	0-0	1-2	2-1	3-0	2-1	0-1	2-3	0-2	1-1
Crewe Alexandra	2-0	1-2	0-3	3-1	1-1	0-1	5-1	3-1	2-2		2-1	4-3	2-0	0-4	1-0	2-2	1-4	2-1	2-1	1-0	1-3	1-3	1-1	2-3
Doncaster Rovers	1-1	0-0	3-3	3-0	1-0	0-1	1-2	0-2	1-0	3-1		1-2	3-0	0-0	1-2	2-2	1-0	1-1	1-0	3-2	2-2	2-2	0-0	0-0
Gillingham	1-1	2-2	1-0	2-1	0-1	1-0	2-0	2-1	2-1	1-0	0-2		2-1	2-1	2-1	0-1	0-1	0-3	3-2	1-0	0-2	3-1	2-0	0-2
Huddersfield Town	2-2	0-2	2-0	0-2	0-3	2-1	2-1	2-0	1-1	1-2	0-0	3-1		3-1	4-2	1-1	1-1	0-3	2-2	3-0	1-1	3-2	2-2	2-3
Leyton Orient	3-2	0-1	1-2	1-1	1-4	1-1	1-1	2-0	0-0	1-1	1-1	3-3	1-0		2-0	0-2	1-3	2-2	2-1	2-3	2-2	0-1	3-1	0-0
Millwall	1-0	0-0	2-0	1-1	0-1	1-0	2-0	2-0	2-1	2-2	2-2	4-1	0-0	2-5		0-1	1-0	1-0	1-1	4-0	0-1	2-0	2-2	1-1
Northampton Town	3-1	1-1	0-0	0-1	0-2	1-3	3-2	2-0	1-0	1-2	0-2	1-1	1-1	0-1	3-0		0-1	2-3	0-2	3-0	2-1	1-0	1-3	1-1
Nottingham Forest	3-0	1-1	1-0	2-0	2-1	1-0	3-0	4-0	0-0	0-1	1-0	5-1	1-3	3-1	1-0			0-2	3-0	1-1	0-4	3-1	1-1	1-0
Oldham Athletic	1-2	0-1	2-0	3-0	1-1	0-3	0-0	0-2	1-0	1-0	4-0	4-1	1-1	3-3	1-2	3-0	5-0		0-1	2-1	1-0	1-0	1-0	1-0
Port Vale	2-1	2-1	0-1	1-0	2-1	0-2	0-2	1-1	3-2	3-0	1-2	2-0	1-2	3-0	2-0	1-0	1-1	3-0		1-3	0-0	0-2	2-3	4-2
Rotherham United	0-2	1-0	4-1	2-0	0-1	1-1	0-1	2-4	0-1	5-1	0-0	3-2	2-3	2-2	2-3	1-2	1-1	2-3	1-5		2-1	1-2	2-1	3-2
Scunthorpe United	3-2	1-3	2-0	1-1	1-2	1-0	3-0	1-0	1-0	2-2	2-0	3-1	2-0	3-1	3-0	1-1	1-1	3-0	1-0			2-2	1-1	1-0
Swansea City	4-2	3-6	1-0	2-0	2-1	0-0	5-0	1-2	2-0	2-1	2-0	2-0	1-2	0-0	2-0	2-1	0-0	0-1	3-0	1-1	0-2		0-0	1-1
Tranmere Rovers	1-0	2-0	1-1	3-1	2-1	1-0	0-2	2-2	1-0	1-0	1-0	2-3	2-2	3-0	3-1	1-1	0-0	1-0	1-2	2-1	0-2	0-2		2-1
Yeovil Town	0-0	0-1	0-0	1-0	2-0	2-1	2-1	0-1	1-0	2-0	1-0	2-0	3-1	2-1	0-1	0-0	0-1	1-0	1-0	1-0	0-2	1-0	0-2	

Football League League Two 2006/2007 Season	Accrington Stanley	Barnet	Boston United	Bristol Rovers	Bury	Chester City	Darlington	Grimsby Town	Hartlepool United	Hereford United	Lincoln City	Macclesfield Town	Mansfield Town	Milton Keynes Dons	Notts County	Peterborough United	Rochdale	Shrewsbury Town	Stockport County	Swindon Town	Torquay United	Walsall	Wrexham
Accrington Stanley		2-1	2-1	1-1	1-1	0-1	0-2	4-1	1-2	2-0	2-2	3-2	3-2	3-4	1-2	3-2	1-1	3-3	0-1	1-1	1-0	1-2	5-
Barnet	1-2		3-3	1-1	2-1	1-0	2-1	0-1	2-1	3-0	0-5	1-0	2-1	3-3	2-3	1-0	3-2	0-0	3-1	1-0	0-1	1-1	1-
Boston United	1-0	2-1		2-1	0-1	1-0	4-1	0-6	0-1	1-1	1-0	4-1	1-1	0-1	3-3	0-1	0-3	0-3	2-1	1-3	1-1	1-1	4-
Bristol Rovers	4-0	2-0	1-0		2-0	0-0	1-2	1-0	0-2	2-1	0-0	0-0	1-0	1-1	2-0	3-2	0-0	1-0	2-1	1-0	1-0	1-2	0-
Bury	2-2	2-2	2-1	0-2		1-3	1-1	3-0	0-1	2-2	2-2	1-1	1-1	0-2	0-1	0-3	0-1	1-2	2-0	0-1	0-1	1-2	1-
Chester City	2-0	2-0	3-1	2-0	1-0		1-1	0-2	2-1	1-1	4-1	0-3	1-1	0-3	0-0	1-1	0-1	0-0	1-1	0-2	1-1	0-0	1-
Darlington	2-1	2-0	2-0	1-1	1-0	1-0		2-2	0-3	1-0	1-1	4-0	0-2	1-0	3-1	0-5	1-2	0-5	1-2	1-1	0-0	1-	
Grimsby Town	2-0	5-0	3-2	4-3	2-0	0-2	0-1		1-4	2-1	0-0	1-1	1-1	1-3	0-2	0-2	0-4	2-1	0-1	1-0	2-0	2-1	2-
Hartlepool United	1-0	0-1	2-1	1-2	2-0	3-0	0-0	2-0		3-2	1-1	3-2	2-0	1-0	1-1	1-0	1-0	0-3	1-1	0-1	1-1	3-1	3-
Hereford United	1-0	2-0	3-0	0-0	1-0	2-0	1-1	0-1	3-1		1-2	1-0	1-3	0-0	3-2	0-0	0-0	0-1	0-2	0-0	1-1	0-1	2-
Lincoln City	3-1	1-0	2-1	1-0	0-2	2-0	1-3	2-0	2-0	1-4		2-1	1-2	2-3	1-1	1-0	7-1	1-1	0-0	2-3	1-0	2-2	0-
Macclesfield Town	3-3	2-3	2-3	0-1	2-3	1-1	1-1	2-1	0-0	3-0	2-1		2-3	1-2	1-1	2-1	1-0	2-2	2-0	2-1	3-3	0-2	2-
Mansfield Town	2-2	2-1	1-2	0-1	0-2	2-1	1-0	1-2	4-1	2-4	1-2			2-1	2-2	0-1	2-1	1-1	1-1	2-0	5-0	2-1	3-
Milton Keynes Dons	3-1	3-1	3-2	2-0	2-1	1-2	1-0	1-2	0-0	1-3	2-2	3-0	1-1		3-2	2-0	2-1	2-0	2-0	0-1	3-2	1-1	2-1
Notts County	3-2	1-1	2-0	1-2	0-1	1-2	0-1	2-0	0-0	0-1	3-1	1-2	0-0	2-2		0-0	1-2	1-1	1-0	5-2	1-2	2-1	
Peterborough United	4-2	1-1	1-1	4-1	0-1	0-2	1-3	2-2	3-5	3-0	1-2	3-1	2-0	4-0	2-0		3-3	2-1	0-3	1-1	5-2	0-2	3-0
Rochdale	4-2	0-2	4-0	0-1	1-3	0-0	0-0	1-0	2-0	1-1	2-0	5-0	2-0	5-0	0-1	0-1		1-1	1-3	0-0	2-0	0-1	2-2
Shrewsbury Town	2-1	0-1	5-0	0-0	1-3	2-1	2-2	2-2	1-1	3-0	0-1	2-1	2-2	2-1	2-0	2-1	3-0		4-2	1-2	1-0	1-1	0-
Stockport County	1-1	2-0	2-0	2-1	0-0	2-0	5-2	3-0	3-3	0-2	2-0	1-1	1-0	1-2	2-0	0-1	2-7	0-3		3-0	1-0	1-0	5-
Swindon Town	2-0	2-1	1-1	2-1	2-1	1-0	3-0	0-1	1-2	2-0	2-0	2-1	1-1	0-1	1-0	2-1	2-0	2-1	2-0		2-1	1-1	2-
Torquay United	0-2	1-1	0-1	0-0	2-2	2-2	0-1	4-1	0-1	0-0	1-2	0-1	1-0	0-2	0-1	1-1	1-0	0-0	1-0	0-1		1-2	1-1
Walsall	3-2	4-1	1-1	2-2	0-1	1-0	1-0	2-0	2-0	1-0	1-2	2-0	4-0	0-0	2-1	5-0	1-1	1-0	2-0	0-2	1-0		1-0
Wrexham	1-3	1-1	3-1	2-0	1-1	0-0	1-0	3-0	1-1	1-0	2-1	0-0	0-0	1-2	0-1	0-0	1-2	1-3	0-1	2-1	1-0	1-1	
Wycombe Wanderers	1-1	1-1	0-0	0-1	3-0	1-0	1-0	1-1	0-1	0-0	1-3	3-0	1-0	0-2	0-0	2-0	1-1	1-1	2-0	1-1	2-0	0-0	1-1

F.A. Premier League
Season 2006/2007

Manchester United	38	28	5	5	83	27	89
Chelsea	38	24	11	3	64	24	83
Liverpool	38	20	8	10	57	27	68
Arsenal	38	19	11	8	63	35	68
Tottenham Hotspur	38	17	9	12	57	54	60
Everton	38	15	13	10	52	36	58
Bolton Wanderers	38	16	8	14	47	52	56
Reading	38	16	7	15	52	47	55
Portsmouth	38	14	12	12	45	42	54
Blackburn Rovers	38	15	7	16	52	54	52
Aston Villa	38	11	17	10	43	41	50
Middlesbrough	38	12	10	16	44	49	46
Newcastle United	38	11	10	17	38	47	43
Manchester City	38	11	9	18	29	44	42
West Ham United	38	12	5	21	35	59	41
Fulham	38	8	15	15	38	60	39
Wigan Athletic	38	10	8	20	37	59	38
Sheffield United	38	10	8	20	32	55	38
Charlton Athletic	38	8	10	20	34	60	34
Watford	38	5	13	20	29	59	28

Champions: Manchester United

Relegated: Sheffield United, Charlton Athletic and Watford

Football League – The Championship
Season 2006/2007

Sunderland	46	27	7	12	76	47	88
Birmingham City	46	26	8	12	67	42	86
Derby County	46	25	9	12	62	46	84
West Bromwich Albion	46	22	10	14	81	55	76
Wolverhampton Wndrs	46	22	10	14	59	56	76
Southampton	46	21	12	13	77	53	75
Preston North End	46	22	8	16	64	53	74
Stoke City	46	19	16	11	62	41	73
Sheffield Wednesday	46	20	11	15	70	66	71
Colchester United	46	20	9	17	70	56	69
Plymouth Argyle	46	17	16	13	63	62	67
Crystal Palace	46	18	11	17	59	51	65
Cardiff City	46	17	13	16	57	53	64
Ipswich Town	46	18	8	20	64	59	62
Burnley	46	15	12	19	52	49	57
Norwich City	46	16	9	21	56	71	57
Coventry City	46	16	8	22	47	62	56
Queens Park Rangers	46	14	11	21	54	68	53
Leicester City	46	13	14	19	49	64	53
Barnsley	46	15	5	26	53	85	50
Hull City	46	13	10	23	51	67	49
Southend United	46	10	12	24	47	80	42
Luton Town	46	10	10	26	53	81	40
Leeds United	46	13	7	26	46	72	36

Leeds United had 10 points deducted

Promotion Play-offs

Southampton .... 1 Derby County 2
Wolverhampton Wanderers ... 2 West Bromwich Albion 3

Derby County .... 2 Southampton .... 3 (aet)
Derby County won 4-3 on penalties
West Bromwich Albion .... 1 Wolverhampton Wanderers ... 0
West Bromwich Albion won 4-2 on aggregate

Derby County .... 1 West Bromwich Albion 0

Promoted: Sunderland, Birmingham City and Derby County

Relegated: Southend United, Luton Town and Leeds United

Football League – League One

Season 2006/2007

Scunthorpe United	46	26	13	7	73	35	91
Bristol City	46	25	10	11	63	39	85
Blackpool	46	24	11	11	76	49	83
Nottingham Forest	46	23	13	10	65	41	82
Yeovil Town	46	23	10	13	55	39	79
Oldham Athletic	46	21	12	13	69	47	75
Swansea City	46	20	12	14	69	53	72
Carlisle United	46	19	11	16	54	55	68
Tranmere Rovers	46	18	13	15	58	53	67
Millwall	46	19	9	18	59	62	66
Doncaster Rovers	46	16	15	15	52	47	63
Port Vale	46	18	6	22	64	65	60
Crewe Alexandra	46	17	9	20	66	72	60
Northampton Town	46	15	14	17	48	51	59
Huddersfield Town	46	14	17	15	60	69	59
Gillingham	46	17	8	21	56	77	59
Cheltenham Town	46	15	9	22	49	61	54
Brighton & Hove Albion	46	14	11	21	49	58	53
AFC Bournemouth	46	13	13	20	50	64	52
Leyton Orient	46	12	15	19	61	77	51
Chesterfield	46	12	11	23	45	53	47
Bradford City	46	11	14	21	47	65	47
Rotherham United	46	13	9	24	58	75	38
Brentford	46	8	13	25	40	79	37

Rotherham United had 10 points deducted

Promotion Play-offs

Oldham Athletic 1	Blackpool 2
Yeovil Town 0	Nottingham Forest 2

Blackpool 3	Oldham Athletic 1
Blackpool won 5-2 on aggregate	
Nottingham Forest 2	Yeovil Town 5
Yeovil Town won 5-4 on aggregate	

Yeovil Town 0	Blackpool 2

Promoted: Scunthorpe United, Bristol City and Blackpool

Relegated: Chesterfield, Bradford City, Rotherham United and Brentford

Football League – League Two

Season 2006/2007

Walsall	46	25	14	7	66	34	89
Hartlepool United	46	26	10	10	65	40	88
Swindon Town	46	25	10	11	58	38	85
Milton Keynes Dons	46	25	9	12	76	58	84
Lincoln City	46	21	11	14	70	59	74
Bristol Rovers	46	20	12	14	49	42	72
Shrewsbury Town	46	18	17	11	68	46	71
Stockport County	46	21	8	17	65	54	71
Rochdale	46	18	12	16	70	50	66
Peterborough United	46	18	11	17	70	61	65
Darlington	46	17	14	15	52	56	65
Wycombe Wanderers	46	16	14	16	52	47	62
Notts County	46	16	14	16	55	53	62
Barnet	46	16	11	19	55	70	59
Grimsby Town	46	17	8	21	57	73	59
Hereford United	46	14	13	19	45	53	55
Mansfield Town	46	14	12	20	58	63	54
Chester City	46	13	14	19	40	48	53
Wrexham	46	13	12	21	43	65	51
Accrington Stanley	46	13	11	22	70	81	50
Bury	46	13	11	22	46	61	50
Macclesfield Town	46	12	12	22	55	77	48
Boston United	46	12	10	24	51	80	46
Torquay United	46	7	14	25	36	63	35

Promotion Play-offs

Bristol Rovers 2	Lincoln City 1
Shrewsbury Town 0	Milton Keynes Dons 0

Lincoln City 3	Bristol Rovers 5
Bristol Rovers won 7-4 on aggregate	
Milton Keynes Dons 1	Shrewsbury Town 2
Shrewsbury Town won 2-1 on aggregate	

Bristol Rovers 3	Shrewsbury Town 1

Promoted: Walsall, Hartlepool United, Swindon Town and Bristol Rovers

Relegated: Boston United and Torquay United

F.A. Cup 2006/2007

Round	Date	Home	Score	Away	Score	
Round 1	11th Nov 2006	Barrow	2	Bristol Rovers	3	
Round 1	11th Nov 2006	Bishop's Stortford	3	King's Lynn	5	
Round 1	11th Nov 2006	Bournemouth	4	Boston United	0	
Round 1	11th Nov 2006	Bradford City	4	Crewe Alexandra	0	
Round 1	11th Nov 2006	Brentford	0	Doncaster Rovers	1	
Round 1	11th Nov 2006	Brighton & Hove Albion	8	Northwich Victoria	0	
Round 1	11th Nov 2006	Burton Albion	1	Tamworth	2	
Round 1	11th Nov 2006	Chelmsford City	1	Aldershot Town	1	
Round 1	10th Nov 2006	Cheltenham Town	0	Scunthorpe United	0	
Round 1	11th Nov 2006	Chesterfield	0	Basingstoke Town	1	
Round 1	11th Nov 2006	Clevedon Town	1	Chester City	4	
Round 1	11th Nov 2006	Exeter City	1	Stockport County	2	
Round 1	12th Nov 2006	Farsley Celtic	0	Milton Keynes Dons	0	
Round 1	11th Nov 2006	Gainsborough Trinity	1	Barnet	3	
Round 1	11th Nov 2006	Gillingham	4	Bromley	1	
Round 1	13th Nov 2006	Havant & Waterlooville	1	Millwall	2	
Round 1	11th Nov 2006	Huddersfield Town	0	Blackpool	1	
Round 1	11th Nov 2006	Kettering Town	3	Oldham Athletic	4	
Round 1	11th Nov 2006	Lewes	1	Darlington	4	
Round 1	11th Nov 2006	Leyton Orient	2	Notts County	1	
Round 1	13th Nov 2006	Macclesfield Town	0	Walsall	0	
Round 1	11th Nov 2006	Mansfield Town	1	Accrington Stanley	0	
Round 1	11th Nov 2006	Morecambe	2	Kidderminster Harriers	1	
Round 1	11th Nov 2006	Newport County	1	Swansea City	3	
Round 1	11th Nov 2006	Northampton Town	0	Grimsby Town	0	
Round 1	11th Nov 2006	Nottingham Forest	5	Yeading	0	
Round 1	11th Nov 2006	Peterborough United	3	Rotherham United	0	
Round 1	11th Nov 2006	Port Vale	2	Lincoln City	1	
Round 1	11th Nov 2006	Rochdale	1	Hartlepool United	1	
Round 1	11th Nov 2006	Rushden & Diamonds	3	Yeovil Town	1	
Round 1	11th Nov 2006	Salisbury City	3	Fleetwood Town	0	
Round 1	11th Nov 2006	Shrewsbury Town	0	Hereford United	0	
Round 1	11th Nov 2006	Stafford Rangers	1	Maidenhead United	1	
Round 1	11th Nov 2006	Swindon Town	3	Carlisle United	1	
Round 1	11th Nov 2006	Torquay United	2	Leatherhead	1	
Round 1	11th Nov 2006	Tranmere Rovers	4	Woking	2	
Round 1	12th Nov 2006	Weymouth	2	Bury	2	
Round 1	11th Nov 2006	Wrexham	1	Stevenage Borough	0	
Round 1	11th Nov 2006	Wycombe Wanderers	2	Oxford United	1	
Round 1	11th Nov 2006	York City	0	Bristol City	1	
Replay	21st Nov 2006	Aldershot Town	2	Chelmsford City	0	
Replay	21st Nov 2006	Bury	4	Weymouth	3	
Replay	21st Nov 2006	Grimsby Town	0	Northampton Town	2	
Replay	20th Nov 2006	Hartlepool United	0	Rochdale	0	(aet)
		Hartlepool United won on penalties				
Replay	21st Nov 2006	Hereford United	2	Shrewsbury Town	0	
Replay	21st Nov 2006	Maidenhead United	0	Stafford Rangers	2	
Replay	21st Nov 2006	Milton Keynes Dons	2	Farsley Celtic	0	
Replay	21st Nov 2006	Scunthorpe United	2	Cheltenham Town	0	
Replay	21st Nov 2006	Walsall	0	Macclesfield Town	1	

Round 2	2nd Dec 2006	Aldershot Town	1	Basingstoke Town	1	
Round 2	2nd Dec 2006	Barnet	4	Northampton Town	1	
Round 2	1st Dec 2006	Bradford City	0	Millwall	0	
Round 2	2nd Dec 2006	Brighton & Hove Albion	3	Stafford Rangers	0	
Round 2	3rd Dec 2006	Bristol City	4	Gillingham	3	
Round 2	2nd Dec 2006	Bristol Rovers	1	Bournemouth	1	
Round 2	2nd Dec 2006	Bury	2	Chester City	2	
Round 2	2nd Dec 2006	Darlington	1	Swansea City	3	
Round 2	2nd Dec 2006	Hereford United	4	Port Vale	0	
Round 2	1st Dec 2006	King's Lynn	0	Oldham Athletic	2	
Round 2	2nd Dec 2006	Macclesfield Town	2	Hartlepool United	1	
Round 2	2nd Dec 2006	Mansfield Town	1	Doncaster Rovers	1	
Round 2	2nd Dec 2006	Milton Keynes Dons	0	Blackpool	2	
Round 2	2nd Dec 2006	Rushden & Diamonds	1	Tamworth	2	
Round 2	2nd Dec 2006	Salisbury City	1	Nottingham Forest	1	
Round 2	3rd Dec 2006	Scunthorpe United	0	Wrexham	2	
Round 2	2nd Dec 2006	Stockport County	2	Wycombe Wanderers	1	
Round 2	1st Dec 2006	Swindon Town	1	Morecambe	0	
Round 2	2nd Dec 2006	Torquay United	1	Leyton Orient	1	
Round 2	2nd Dec 2006	Tranmere Rovers	1	Peterborough United	2	
Replay	12th Dec 2006	Basingstoke Town	1	Aldershot Town	3	
Replay	12th Dec 2006	Bournemouth	0	Bristol Rovers	1	
Replay	12th Dec 2006	Chester City	1	Bury	3	
		Bury were disqualified after fielding an ineligible player				
Replay	12th Dec 2006	Doncaster Rovers	2	Mansfield Town	0	
Replay	12th Dec 2006	Leyton Orient	1	Torquay United	2	
Replay	12th Dec 2006	Millwall	1	Bradford City	0	(aet)
Replay	12th Dec 2006	Nottingham Forest	2	Salisbury City	0	
Round 3	9th Jan 2007	Barnet	2	Colchester United	1	
Round 3	6th Jan 2007	Birmingham City	2	Newcastle United	2	
Round 3	6th Jan 2007	Blackpool	4	Aldershot Town	2	
Round 3	6th Jan 2007	Bristol City	3	Coventry City	3	
Round 3	5th Jan 2007	Bristol Rovers	1	Hereford United	0	
Round 3	7th Jan 2007	Cardiff City	0	Tottenham Hotspur	0	
Round 3	6th Jan 2007	Chelsea	6	Macclesfield Town	1	
Round 3	6th Jan 2007	Chester City	0	Ipswich Town	0	
Round 3	6th Jan 2007	Crystal Palace	2	Swindon Town	1	
Round 3	6th Jan 2007	Derby County	3	Wrexham	1	
Round 3	6th Jan 2007	Doncaster Rovers	0	Bolton Wanderers	4	
Round 3	7th Jan 2007	Everton	1	Blackburn Rovers	4	
Round 3	6th Jan 2007	Hull City	1	Middlesbrough	1	
Round 3	6th Jan 2007	Leicester City	2	Fulham	2	
Round 3	6th Jan 2007	Liverpool	1	Arsenal	3	
Round 3	7th Jan 2007	Manchester United	2	Aston Villa	1	
Round 3	6th Jan 2007	Nottingham Forest	2	Charlton Athletic	0	
Round 3	6th Jan 2007	Peterborough United	1	Plymouth Argyle	1	
Round 3	6th Jan 2007	Portsmouth	2	Wigan Athletic	1	
Round 3	6th Jan 2007	Preston North End	1	Sunderland	0	
Round 3	6th Jan 2007	Queen's Park Rangers	2	Luton Town	2	
Round 3	9th Jan 2007	Reading	3	Burnley	2	
Round 3	6th Jan 2007	Sheffield United	0	Swansea City	3	
Round 3	7th Jan 2007	Sheffield Wednesday	1	Manchester City	1	
Round 3	6th Jan 2007	Southend United	1	Barnsley	1	

Round	Date	Home		Away		
Round 3	5th Jan 2007	Stoke City	2	Millwall	0	
Round 3	6th Jan 2007	Tamworth	1	Norwich City	4	
Round 3	6th Jan 2007	Torquay United	0	Southampton	2	
Round 3	6th Jan 2007	Watford	4	Stockport County	1	
Round 3	6th Jan 2007	West Bromwich Albion	3	Leeds United	1	
Round 3	6th Jan 2007	West Ham United	3	Brighton & Hove Albion	0	
Round 3	6th Jan 2007	Wolverhampton Wanderers	2	Oldham Athletic	2	
Replay	16th Jan 2007	Barnsley	0	Southend United	2	
Replay	16th Jan 2007	Coventry City	0	Bristol City	2	
Replay	17th Jan 2007	Fulham	4	Leicester City	3	
Replay	16th Jan 2007	Ipswich Town	1	Chester City	0	
Replay	23rd Jan 2007	Luton Town	1	Queen's Park Rangers	0	
Replay	16th Jan 2007	Manchester City	2	Sheffield Wednesday	1	
Replay	16th Jan 2007	Middlesbrough	4	Hull City	3	
Replay	17th Jan 2007	Newcastle United	1	Birmingham City	5	
Replay	16th Jan 2007	Oldham Athletic	0	Wolverhampton Wanderers	2	
Replay	16th Jan 2007	Plymouth Argyle	2	Peterborough United	1	
Replay	17th Jan 2007	Tottenham Hotspur	4	Cardiff City	0	
Round 4	28th Jan 2007	Arsenal	1	Bolton Wanderers	1	
Round 4	27th Jan 2007	Barnet	0	Plymouth Argyle	2	
Round 4	27th Jan 2007	Birmingham City	2	Reading	3	
Round 4	27th Jan 2007	Blackpool	1	Norwich City	1	
Round 4	27th Jan 2007	Bristol City	2	Middlesbrough	2	
Round 4	28th Jan 2007	Chelsea	3	Nottingham Forest	0	
Round 4	27th Jan 2007	Crystal Palace	0	Preston North End	2	
Round 4	27th Jan 2007	Derby County	1	Bristol Rovers	0	
Round 4	27th Jan 2007	Fulham	3	Stoke City	0	
Round 4	27th Jan 2007	Ipswich Town	1	Swansea City	0	
Round 4	27th Jan 2007	Luton Town	0	Blackburn Rovers	4	
Round 4	28th Jan 2007	Manchester City	3	Southampton	1	
Round 4	27th Jan 2007	Manchester United	2	Portsmouth	1	
Round 4	27th Jan 2007	Tottenham Hotspur	3	Southend United	1	
Round 4	27th Jan 2007	West Ham United	0	Watford	1	
Round 4	28th Jan 2007	Wolverhampton Wanderers	0	West Bromwich Albion	3	
Replay	14th Feb 2007	Bolton Wanderers	1	Arsenal	3	(aet)
Replay	13th Feb 2007	Middlesbrough	2	Bristol City	2	(aet)
		Middlesbrough won on penalties				
Replay	13th Feb 2007	Norwich City	3	Blackpool	2	(aet)
Round 5	17th Feb 2007	Arsenal	0	Blackburn Rovers	0	
Round 5	17th Feb 2007	Chelsea	4	Norwich City	0	
Round 5	18th Feb 2007	Fulham	0	Tottenham Hotspur	4	
Round 5	17th Feb 2007	Manchester United	1	Reading	1	
Round 5	17th Feb 2007	Middlesbrough	2	West Bromwich Albion	2	
Round 5	17th Feb 2007	Plymouth Argyle	2	Derby County	0	
Round 5	18th Feb 2007	Preston North End	1	Manchester City	3	
Round 5	17th Feb 2007	Watford	1	Ipswich Town	0	
Replay	28th Feb 2007	Blackburn Rovers	1	Arsenal	0	
Replay	27th Feb 2007	Reading	2	Manchester United	3	
Replay	27th Feb 2007	West Bromwich Albion	1	Middlesbrough	1	(aet)
		Middlesbrough won on penalties				

Round 6	11th Mar 2007	Blackburn Rovers	2	Manchester City	0	
Round 6	11th Mar 2007	Chelsea	3	Tottenham Hotspur	3	
Round 6	10th Mar 2007	Middlesbrough	2	Manchester United	2	
Round 6	11th Mar 2007	Plymouth Argyle	0	Watford	1	
Replay	19th Mar 2007	Manchester United	1	Middlesbrough	0	
Replay	19th Mar 2007	Tottenham Hotspur	1	Chelsea	2	
Semi-Final	15th Apr 2007	Chelsea	2	Blackburn Rovers	1	(aet)
Semi-Final	14th Apr 2007	Manchester United	4	Watford	1	
FINAL	19th May 2007	Chelsea	1	Manchester United	0	(aet)

Football League Cup 2006/2007

Round	Date	Home	Score	Away	Score	
Round 1	21st Aug 2006	Accrington Stanley	1	Nottingham Forest	0	
Round 1	22nd Aug 2006	Birmingham City	1	Shrewsbury Town	0	
Round 1	22nd Aug 2006	Blackpool	2	Barnsley	2	(aet)
		Barnsley won on penalties				
Round 1	22nd Aug 2006	Bournemouth	1	Southend United	3	
Round 1	23rd Aug 2006	Brighton & Hove Albion	1	Boston United	0	
Round 1	22nd Aug 2006	Bristol Rovers	1	Luton Town	1	(aet)
		Luton Town won on penalties				
Round 1	22nd Aug 2006	Burnley	0	Hartlepool United	1	
Round 1	22nd Aug 2006	Bury	2	Sunderland	0	
Round 1	22nd Aug 2006	Cardiff City	0	Barnet	2	
Round 1	22nd Aug 2006	Carlisle United	1	Bradford City	1	(aet)
		Carlisle United won on penalties				
Round 1	22nd Aug 2006	Cheltenham Town	2	Bristol City	1	
Round 1	23rd Aug 2006	Chesterfield	0	Wolverhampton Wanderers	0	(aet)
		Chesterfield won on penalties				
Round 1	22nd Aug 2006	Crystal Palace	1	Notts County	2	
Round 1	22nd Aug 2006	Doncaster Rovers	3	Rochdale	2	
Round 1	22nd Aug 2006	Grimsby Town	0	Crewe Alexandra	3	
Round 1	22nd Aug 2006	Hereford United	3	Coventry City	1	
Round 1	22nd Aug 2006	Huddersfield Town	0	Mansfield Town	2	
Round 1	22nd Aug 2006	Hull City	2	Tranmere Rovers	1	(aet)
Round 1	22nd Aug 2006	Leeds United	1	Chester City	0	
Round 1	22nd Aug 2006	Leicester City	2	Macclesfield	0	
Round 1	24th Aug 2006	Leyton Orient	0	West Bromwich Albion	3	
Round 1	22nd Aug 2006	Millwall	2	Gillingham	1	
Round 1	22nd Aug 2006	MiltonKeynes Dons	1	Colchester United	0	(aet)
Round 1	22nd Aug 2006	Peterborough United	2	Ipswich Town	2	(aet)
		Peterborough United won on penalties				
Round 1	22nd Aug 2006	Plymouth Argyle	0	Walsall	1	
Round 1	23rd Aug 2006	Port Vale	2	Preston North End	1	
Round 1	22nd Aug 2006	Queen's Park Rangers	3	Northampton Town	2	
Round 1	22nd Aug 2006	Rotherham United	3	Oldham Athletic	1	
Round 1	22nd Aug 2006	Scunthorpe United	4	Lincoln City	3	(aet)
Round 1	23rd Aug 2006	Sheffield Wednesday	1	Wrexham	4	
Round 1	23rd Aug 2006	Southampton	5	Yeovil Town	2	
Round 1	22nd Aug 2006	Stockport County	0	Derby County	1	
Round 1	22nd Aug 2006	Stoke City	1	Darlington	2	
Round 1	22nd Aug 2006	Swansea City	2	Wycombe Wanderers	3	(aet)
Round 1	22nd Aug 2006	Swindon Town	2	Brentford	2	(aet)
		Brentford won on penalties				
Round 1	23rd Aug 2006	Torquay United	0	Norwich City	2	
Round 2	19th Sep 2006	Barnsley	1	MiltonKeynes Dons	2	
Round 2	19th Sep 2006	Birmingham City	4	Wrexham	1	(aet)
Round 2	19th Sep 2006	Brentford	0	Luton Town	3	
Round 2	19th Sep 2006	Charlton Athletic	1	Carlisle United	0	
Round 2	20th Sep 2006	Chesterfield	2	Manchester City	1	
Round 2	19th Sep 2006	Crewe Alexandra	2	Wigan Athletic	0	
Round 2	20th Sep 2006	Doncaster Rovers	3	Derby County	3	(aet)
		Doncaster Rovers won on penalties				
Round 2	20th Sep 2006	Fulham	1	Wycombe Wanderers	2	
Round 2	19th Sep 2006	Hereford United	1	Leicester City	3	
Round 2	19th Sep 2006	Hull City	0	Hartlepool United	0	(aet)
		Hull City won on penalties				
Round 2	19th Sep 2006	Leeds United	3	Barnet	1	

Round 2	19th Sep 2006	Mansfield Town	1	Portsmouth	2	
Round 2	20th Sep 2006	Middlesbrough	0	Notts County	1	
Round 2	19th Sep 2006	Millwall	0	Southampton	4	
Round 2	19th Sep 2006	Peterborough United	1	Everton	2	
Round 2	19th Sep 2006	Port Vale	3	Queen's Park Rangers	2	
Round 2	19th Sep 2006	Reading	3	Darlington	3	(aet)
		Reading won on penalties				
Round 2	19th Sep 2006	Rotherham United	2	Norwich City	4	
Round 2	20th Sep 2006	Scunthorpe United	1	Aston Villa	2	
Round 2	19th Sep 2006	Sheffield United	1	Bury	0	
Round 2	19th Sep 2006	Southend United	3	Brighton & Hove Albion	2	
Round 2	19th Sep 2006	Walsall	1	Bolton Wanderers	3	
Round 2	19th Sep 2006	Watford	0	Accrington Stanley	0	(aet)
		Watford won on penalties				
Round 2	19th Sep 2006	West Bromwich Albion	3	Cheltenham Town	1	
Round 3	25th Oct 2006	Blackburn Rovers	0	Chelsea	2	
Round 3	25th Oct 2006	Charlton Athletic	1	Bolton Wanderers	0	
Round 3	24th Oct 2006	Chesterfield	2	West Ham United	1	
Round 3	25th Oct 2006	Crewe Alexandra	1	Manchester United	2	(aet)
Round 3	24th Oct 2006	Everton	4	Luton Town	0	
Round 3	24th Oct 2006	Leeds United	1	Southend United	3	
Round 3	24th Oct 2006	Leicester City	2	Aston Villa	3	(aet)
Round 3	25th Oct 2006	Liverpool	4	Reading	3	
Round 3	25th Oct 2006	MiltonKeynes Dons	0	Tottenham Hotspur	5	
Round 3	25th Oct 2006	Newcastle United	3	Portsmouth	0	
Round 3	24th Oct 2006	Notts County	2	Southampton	0	
Round 3	24th Oct 2006	Port Vale	0	Norwich City	0	(aet)
		Port Vale won on penalties				
Round 3	24th Oct 2006	Sheffield United	2	Birmingham City	4	
Round 3	24th Oct 2006	Watford	2	Hull City	1	
Round 3	24th Oct 2006	West Bromwich Albion	0	Arsenal	2	
Round 3	24th Oct 2006	Wycombe Wanderers	2	Doncaster Rovers	2	(aet)
		Wycombe Wanderers won on penalties				
Round 4	8th Nov 2006	Birmingham City	0	Liverpool	1	
Round 4	8th Nov 2006	Chelsea	4	Aston Villa	0	
Round 4	7th Nov 2006	Chesterfield	3	Charlton Athletic	3	(aet)
		Charlton Athletic won on penalties				
Round 4	8th Nov 2006	Everton	0	Arsenal	1	
Round 4	7th Nov 2006	Notts County	0	Wycombe Wanderers	1	
Round 4	7th Nov 2006	Southend United	1	Manchester United	0	
Round 4	8th Nov 2006	Tottenham Hotspur	3	Port Vale	1	(aet)
Round 4	7th Nov 2006	Watford	2	Newcastle United	2	(aet)
		Newcastle United won on penalties				
Round 5	19th Dec 2006	Charlton Athletic	0	Wycombe Wanderers	1	
Round 5	9th Jan 2007	Liverpool	3	Arsenal	6	
Round 5	20th Dec 2006	Newcastle United	0	Chelsea	1	
Round 5	20th Dec 2006	Tottenham Hotspur	1	Southend United	0	(aet)

SEMI-FINALS

1st leg	24th Jan 2007	Tottenham Hotspur	2	Arsenal	2	
2nd leg	31st Jan 2007	Arsenal	3	Tottenham Hotspur	1	(aet)
		Arsenal won 5-3 on aggregate				
1st leg	10th Jan 2007	Wycombe Wanderers	1	Chelsea	1	
2nd leg	23rd Jan 2007	Chelsea	4	Wycombe Wanderers	0	
		Chelsea won 5-1 on aggregate				
FINAL	25th Feb 2007	Chelsea	2	Arsenal	1	

1st March 2006
v URUGUAY *Anfield, Liverpool*

P. Robinson	Tottenham Hotspur
G. Neville	Manchester United
J. Terry	Chelsea (sub. L. King 46)
R. Ferdinand	Manchester United
W. Bridge	Chelsea (sub. J. Carragher 31)
D. Beckham	Real Madrid
	(sub. S. Wright-Phillips 64)
M. Carrick	Tottenham Hotspur
S. Gerrard	Liverpool (sub. J. Jenas 46)
J. Cole	Chelsea
W. Rooney	Man. United (sub. P. Crouch 64)
D. Bent	Charlton Athletic (sub. J. Defoe 82)

Result 2-1   Crouch, Cole

30th May 2006
v HUNGARY
Old Trafford, Manchester

P. Robinson	Tottenham Hotspur
G. Neville	Man. United (sub. O. Hargreaves 46)
R. Ferdinand	Manchester United
J. Terry	Chelsea (sub. S. Campbell 76)
A. Cole	Arsenal
J. Carragher	Liverpool
D. Beckham	Real Madrid
F. Lampard	Chelsea
J. Cole	Chelsea
S. Gerrard	Liverpool (sub. P. Crouch 65)
M. Owen	Newcastle U. (sub. T. Walcott 65)

Result 3-1   Gerrard, Terry, Crouch

3rd June 2006
v JAMAICA *Old Trafford, Manchester*

P. Robinson	Tottenham H. (sub. D. James 46)
J. Carragher	Liverpool
R. Ferdinand	Manchester United
J. Terry	Chelsea (sub. S. Campbell 33)
A. Cole	Arsenal (sub. W. Bridge 35)
D. Beckham	Real Madrid (sub. A. Lennon 68)
S. Gerrard	Liverpool (sub. S. Downing 77)
F. Lampard	Chelsea (sub. M. Carrick 68)
J. Cole	Chelsea
M. Owen	Newcastle United
P. Crouch	Liverpool

Result 6-0   Lampard, Taylor (og), Crouch 3, Owen

10th June 2006
v PARAGUAY (WC)
Frankfurt-am-Main

P. Robinson	Tottenham Hotspur
G. Neville	Manchester United
R. Ferdinand	Manchester United
J. Terry	Chelsea
A. Cole	Arsenal
D. Beckham	Real Madrid
S. Gerrard	Liverpool
F. Lampard	Chelsea
J. Cole	Chelsea (sub. O. Hargreaves 83)
M. Owen	Newcastle U. (sub. S. Downing 56)
P. Crouch	Liverpool

Result 1-0   Gamarra (og)

15th June 2006
v TRINIDAD & TOBAGO (WC)
Nuremberg

P. Robinson	Tottenham Hotspur
J. Carragher	Liverpool (sub. A. Lennon 58)
R. Ferdinand	Manchester United
J. Terry	Chelsea
A. Cole	Arsenal
D. Beckham	Manchester United
S. Gerrard	Liverpool
F. Lampard	Chelsea
J. Cole	Chelsea (sub. S. Downing 75)
M. Owen	Newcastle U. (sub. W. Rooney 58)
P. Crouch	Liverpool

Result 2-0   Crouch, Gerrard

20th June 2006
v SWEDEN (WC) *Cologne*

P. Robinson	Tottenham Hotspur
J. Carragher	Liverpool
R. Ferdinand	Man. United (sub. S. Campbell 56)
J. Terry	Chelsea
A. Cole	Arsenal
D. Beckham	Real Madrid
O. Hargreaves	Bayern Munich
F. Lampard	Chelsea
J. Cole	Chelsea
W. Rooney	Man. United (sub. S. Gerrard 69)
M. Owen	Newcastle Utd. (sub. P. Crouch 4)

Result 2-2   J. Cole, Gerrard

25th June 2006
v ECUADOR (WC)   *Stuttgart*

P. Robinson	Tottenham Hotspur
O. Hargreaves	Bayern Munich
J. Terry	Chelsea
R. Ferdinand	Manchester United
A. Cole	Arsenal
M. Carrick	Tottenham Hotspur
D. Beckham	Real Madrid (sub. A. Lennon 87)
S. Gerrard	Liverpool (sub. S. Downing 90)
F. Lampard	Chelsea
J. Cole	Chelsea (sub. J. Carragher 77)
W. Rooney	Manchester United

Result 1-0   Beckham

1st July 2006
v PORTUGAL (WC) *Gelsenkirchen*

P. Robinson	Tottenham Hotspur
G. Neville	Manchester United
J. Terry	Chelsea
R. Ferdinand	Manchester United
A. Cole	Arsenal
O. Hargreaves	Bayern Munich
D. Beckham	Real Madrid (sub. A. Lennon 51 (sub. J. Carragher 118))
S. Gerrard	Liverpool
F. Lampard	Chelsea
J. Cole	Chelsea (sub. P. Crouch 65)
W. Rooney	Manchester United

Result 0-0 (aet)   Portugal won 3-1 on penalties

16th August 2006
v GREECE   *Old Trafford*

P. Robinson	Tottenham H. (sub. C. Kirkland 46)
A. Cole	Arsenal (sub. W. Bridge 81)
J. Terry	Chelsea
R. Ferdinand	Manchester United
G. Neville	Man. United (sub. J. Carragher 79)
O. Hargreaves	Bayern Munich
F. Lampard	Chelsea
S. Gerrard	Liverpool (sub. D. Bent 79)
S. Downing	Middlesbrough (sub. K. Richardson 69)
P. Crouch	Liverpool
J. Defoe	Tottenham H. (sub. A. Lennon 69)

Result 4-0   Terry, Lampard, Crouch 2

2nd September 2006
v ANDORRA (ECQ)   *Old Trafford*

P. Robinson	Tottenham Hotspur
W. Brown	Manchester United
J. Terry	Chelsea
A. Cole	Chelsea
P. Neville	Everton (sub. A. Lennon 65)
S. Gerrard	Liverpool
O. Hargreaves	Bayern Munich
F. Lampard	Chelsea
S. Downing	Middlesbrough (sub. K. Richardson 65)
J. Defoe	Tottenham H. (sub. A. Johnson 70)
P. Crouch	Liverpool

Result 5-0   Gerrard, Defoe 2, Crouch 2

6th September 2006
v MACEDONIA (ECQ)   *Skopje*

P. Robinson	Tottenham Hotspur
P. Neville	Everton
A. Cole	Chelsea
R. Ferdinand	Manchester United
J. Terry	Chelsea
S. Gerrard	Liverpool
O. Hargreaves	Bayern Munich
F. Lampard	Chelsea (sub. M. Carrick 85)
S. Downing	Middlesbrough
P. Crouch	Liverpool (sub. A. Johnson 88)
J. Defoe	Tottenham H. (sub. A. Lennon 76)

Result 1-0   Crouch

11th October 2006
v CROATIA (ECQ)   *Zagreb*

P. Robinson	Tottenham Hotspur
G. Neville	Manchester United
A. Cole	Chelsea
J. Carragher	Liverpool (sub. K. Richardson 72)
R. Ferdinand	Manchester United
J. Terry	Chelsea
M. Carrick	Manchester United
F. Lampard	Chelsea
S. Parker	Newcastle United (sub. S. Wright-Phillips 72)
W. Rooney	Manchester United
P. Crouch	Liverpool (sub. J. Defoe 72)

Result 0-2

15th November 2006
v HOLLAND *Amsterdam ArenA*

P. Robinson	Tottenham Hotspur
M. Richards	Manchester City
A. Cole	Chelsea
R. Ferdinand	Manchester United
J. Terry	Chelsea
S. Gerrard	Liverpool
J. Cole	Chelsea (sub. K. Richardson 78)
F. Lampard	Chelsea
M. Carrick	Manchester United
W. Rooney	Manchester United
A. Johnson	Everton (sub. S. Wright-Phillips 74)

Result 1-1   Rooney

7th February 2007
v SPAIN *Old Trafford*

B. Foster	Watford
G. Neville	Man. United (sub. M. Richards 65)
J. Woodgate	Middlesbrough (sub. J. Carragher 65)
R. Ferdinand	Manchester United
P. Neville	Everton (sub. S. Downing 74)
S. Wright-Phillips	Chelsea (sub. J. Defoe 70)
S. Gerrard	Liverpool (sub. G. Barry 45)
M. Carrick	Manchester United
F. Lampard	Chelsea (sub. J. Barton 80)
K. Dyer	Newcastle United
P. Crouch	Liverpool

Result 0-1

24th March 2007
v ISRAEL (ECQ) *Tel Aviv*

P. Robinson	Tottenham Hotspur
P. Neville	Everton (sub. M. Richards 73)
J. Carragher	Liverpool
J. Terry	Chelsea
R. Ferdinand	Manchester United
S. Gerrard	Liverpool
O. Hargreaves	Bayern Munich
F. Lampard	Chelsea
A. Lennon	Tottenham H. (sub. S. Downing 83)
W. Rooney	Manchester United
A. Johnson	Everton (sub. J. Defoe 80)

Result 0-0

28th March 2007
v ANDORRA (ECQ) *Barcelona*

P. Robinson	Tottenham Hotspur
M. Richards	Manchester City (sub. K. Dyer 62)
J. Terry	Chelsea
R. Ferdinand	Manchester United
A. Cole	Chelsea
O. Hargreaves	Bayern Munich
S. Gerrard	Liverpool
A. Lennon	Tottenham Hotspur
S. Downing	Middlesbrough
W. Rooney	Manchester United (sub. J. Defoe 62)
A. Johnson	Everton (sub. D. Nugent 79)

Result 3-0   Gerrard 2, Nugent

1st June 2007
v BRAZIL *Wembley*

P. Robinson	Tottenham Hotspur
J. Carragher	Liverpool
J. Terry	Chelsea (sub. W. Brown 73)
L. King	Tottenham Hotspur
N. Shorey	Reading
S. Gerrard	Liverpool
D. Beckham	Real Madrid (sub. J. Jenas 77)
F. Lampard	Chelsea (sub. M. Carrick 88)
J. Cole	Chelsea (sub. S. Downing 72)
M. Owen	Newcastle United (sub. P. Crouch 82)
A. Smith	Manchester United (sub. K. Dyer 62)

Result 1-1   Terry

6th June 2007
v ESTONIA (ECQ) *Tallinn*

P. Robinson	Tottenham Hotspur
L. King	Tottenham Hotspur
J. Terry	Chelsea
W. Brown	Manchester United
W. Bridge	Chelsea
S. Gerrard	Liverpool
D. Beckham	Real Madrid (sub. K. Dyer 68)
F. Lampard	Chelsea
J. Cole	Chelsea (sub. S. Downing 76)
P. Crouch	Liverpool
M. Owen	Newcastle United (sub. J. Jenas 88)

Result 3-0   Cole, Crouch, Owen

Supporters' Guides Series

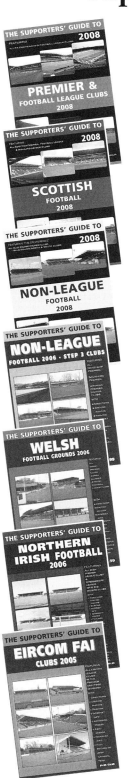

This top-selling series has been published annually since 1982 and the n editions contain 2006/2007 Season's results and tables, Directions, Photos, Phc numbers, Parking information, Admission details, Disabled info and much m

THE SUPPORTERS' GUIDE TO PREMIER & FOOTBALL LEAGUE CLUBS 2008

The 24th edition featuring all Premiership and Football Leag clubs. *Price £6.99*

THE SUPPORTERS' GUIDE TO SCOTTISH FOOTBALL 2008

The 16th edition featuring all Scottish Premier League, Scottish Leag and Highland League clubs. *Price £6.99*

THE SUPPORTERS' GUIDE TO NON-LEAGUE FOOTBALL 2008

This 16th edition covers all 68 clubs in Step 1 & Step 2 of Non-Leag football – the Football Conference National, Conference North a Conference South. *Price £6.99*

THE SUPPORTERS' GUIDE TO NON-LEAGUE FOOTBALL 2007 – STEP 3 CLUBS

Following the reorganisation of Non-League Football the 3rd editi of this book features the 66 clubs which feed into the Footb Conference. *Price £6.99*

THE SUPPORTERS' GUIDE TO WELSH FOOTBALL GROUNDS 2007

The 11th edition featuring all League of Wales, Cymru Alliance & Welsh Fo ball League Clubs + results, tables & much more. *Price £6.99*

THE SUPPORTERS' GUIDE TO NORTHERN IRISH FOOTBALL 2007

This 4th edition features all Irish Premier League and Irish Football Leag Clubs + results, tables & much more. *Price £6.99*

THE SUPPORTERS' GUIDE TO EIRCOM FAI CLUBS 2006

Back after a long absence this 4th edition features all Eircom League Prem and First Division Clubs + 10 years of results, tables & mu more. *Price £6.99*

These books are available UK & Surface post free from –

Soccer Books Limited (Dept. SBL)
72 St. Peter's Avenue
Cleethorpes
N.E. Lincolnshire